I0559510

Courting in the Kingdom

10 Steps to Discern Your Perfect Match

By Karajah Yashar

Orlando, FL 2024

Courting in the Kingdom
10 Steps to Discern Your Perfect Match

www.bspbooks.com

Copyright © 2024 by Blackstone Publishing.

All rights reserved. No part of this publication may be reproduced, distributed, or transmitted in any form or by any means, including photocopying, recording, or other electronic or mechanical methods, including recording or by any information storage and retrieval system, without the prior written permission in writing from the copyright owner. Text produced with ChatGPT.

ISBN: 978-1-962691-32-1

First Edition: June 2024

Dedication

This book is dedicated to all those who have been seeking that special person, their soulmate, their spouse. The journey towards finding true love is often challenging and filled with disappointments. Yet, it is important to keep striving, knowing that each step brings you closer to the person meant for you.

Remember that God knows your desires and needs better than anyone else. He is aware of the longings of your heart and is guiding you through every trial and triumph. Trust in His wisdom and timing, for He has a perfect plan for your life and your relationships.

Your spouse is out there, wanting and seeking you just as much as you are seeking them. May this guide serve as a beacon, illuminating your path towards a fulfilling and loving relationship. Stay patient, keep the faith, and never lose hope in the beautiful journey of finding your true companion.

The Goal of Courtship

The goal of courtship is to determine if this is the right person for you, not to fight to stay together at all costs. Courtship is a time for discernment, where both individuals evaluate compatibility, shared values, and long-term goals. If it becomes clear that you are wellsuited for each other, the focus then shifts to engagement, marriage, and committing to a lifetime together. This transition marks the beginning of a partnership meant to endure 'until death does you part,' built on a foundation of mutual understanding and genuine compatibility discovered during the courtship phase.

Identifying deal breakers is a crucial aspect of this discernment process. These could be fundamental differences in faith, values, life goals, or personality traits that would hinder a harmonious and fulfilling marriage. It's important to address these issues openly and honestly, even if the person has many other admirable qualities. Sometimes, despite strong feelings and affection, it becomes necessary to end the courtship if these deal breakers indicate that you are not meant for each other. Walking away from a relationship that doesn't align with your core values and long-term vision is a sign of wisdom and respect for both yourself and your partner. Ending a courtship can be difficult, but it is sometimes the best decision for ensuring both individuals find the right person to share their lives with.

Table of Contents

My Story

When I was about 12 years old, I experienced a profound moment that shaped my approach to relationships for the rest of my life. I felt the Lord tell me that there is a man for every woman and a woman for every man. It was a comforting revelation, accompanied by a strong sense that I wouldn't have to go out actively searching for my future spouse. Instead, when I met her, I would just know. This assurance stayed with me through my formative years.

During my teenage years, while many of my friends and sisters were dating, I chose to remain single. I watched them navigate the complexities of teenage relationships, but I felt no urgency to join in. As my late teens and early twenties rolled around, I immersed myself in the club and party scene, yet I still never dated. My social outings were always in groups, never one-on-one with a woman. The first part of my twenties was a whirlwind of parties and even a few visits to strip clubs. However, everything changed at age 23 when I experienced a spiritual rebirth. After this pivotal moment, I abandoned my partying lifestyle and began a genuine walk with God. My focus shifted entirely to learning about Him, and I became resolute in my decision to avoid premarital sex, steering clear of situations that could lead to temptation.

One particular incident stands out from this period. A woman I had a huge crush on visited me from New Jersey shortly after I moved to Florida. She had booked a hotel in South Beach Miami, and my friends and I met up with her and her friends. The night went well, and it seemed like the perfect setup for something more to happen. But at the end of the night, as I sat up and put my shoes on, an overwhelming feeling compelled me to leave. I didn't fully understand why at the time, but I felt God was protecting me. This sense of a divine bubble around me continued into my late twenties, when feelings of loneliness would occasionally surface. I felt ready for a wife but remained patient, trusting in God's timing. Although I went on a few dates during this time, they never led to anything beyond enjoyable company. By my early thirties, I sensed that my wife was on the horizon.

In 2010, I met the woman who would become my wife for the next ten years. Everything moved quickly. After just three weeks, I asked her to marry me, and by the fourth week, she was pregnant. We didn't wait until the wedding night to consummate our marriage, but I reasoned that it was okay because we eventually did marry on our six month anniversary of when we met. Our marriage was harmonious, with minimal arguments. However, this was partly due to my exwife's tendency to sweep her issues under the rug. After a decade together, we separated, and four years later, we divorced. Although we still have a great mutual respect for each other today, I realize that if I had applied many of the practical steps outlined in this book, I would have recognized earlier that we were not equally yoked in some critical aspects.

Post-divorce, I entered two six-month relationships. Still grappling with the hurt and confusion from my separation, I deviated from my original ideals for courting. I engaged in premarital sex with my girlfriends, only to feel convicted and stop midway through each relationship. Occasionally, I slipped back into old habits, but I knew this was not a godly approach. During this time, I truly felt the worldly confusion that comes with secular dating, which brought various negative repercussions in my personal life. As I write this book today, I am in the midst of the courting process with a beautiful woman of God, whom I know in my soul I want to marry. She is forty years old and has been faithfully waiting for God to send her husband, rather than giving her body to random men she dates. She reminded me of my earlier conviction not to have sex until marriage.

Early on, we faced some issues because I was not fully living in righteousness, tarnished by my experiences with worldly dating. However, thanks to her influence and the Holy Spirit, clarity finally returned. The difference between kingdom courting and worldly dating is profound. The following chapters will serve as a helpful guide for those genuinely seeking to find their special soulmate, a spouse to stand by their side for life. I pray that this book helps all seekers on their quest for righteous love.

Introduction: Rediscovering Righteous Relationships

In a world where the marriage rate has plummeted from 76.5% in 1970 to just over 31% in 2023, the fabric of our communities and churches is fraying. This stark decline has been felt most acutely among Black and Hispanic women, with marriage rates dropping by 60% and 33% respectively. These numbers are more than just statistics; they represent countless lives grappling with the challenges of finding and maintaining meaningful relationships in a modern landscape fraught with complexity and confusion.

As believers, we know that marriage is not merely a social contract but a divine covenant. It is the foundation upon which families, churches, and communities are built. The erosion of marriage signifies more than a shift in societal norms—it reflects a deeper spiritual malaise.

Our frustration with relationships today stems from a lack of understanding about how to approach them in a way that aligns with God's will. This book seeks to illuminate a path back to the principles that foster healthy, holy, and lasting unions.

The Importance of a God-Centered Approach

To comprehend the gravity of the current state of relationships, we must first understand the significance of marriage in God's design. In Ephesians 5:25-33, the apostle Paul likens marriage to the relationship between Christ and the Church, emphasizing sacrificial love, mutual respect, and unyielding commitment. This divine blueprint sets a high standard, one that modern dating culture often neglects or outright contradicts.

The decline in marriage rates is not just a matter of changing times; it is indicative of a broader departure from these foundational values. The journey back to a place where marriage is revered and pursued begins with courting—an intentional, principled approach to relationships that honors God and seeks His guidance at every step.

Understanding Courtship in a Contemporary Context

Courtship, unlike modern dating, is not about personal gratification or casual experimentation. It is a deliberate process designed to discern God's will for a potential life partner. In contrast to the fleeting and often superficial nature of contemporary dating, courtship emphasizes purpose, purity, and prayer.

In today's world, the concept of courtship might seem antiquated or overly rigid. However, its principles are timeless and adaptable to modern contexts. Courting in the kingdom means more than following a set of rules; it involves cultivating a heart posture that prioritizes spiritual compatibility and long-term commitment over momentary attraction and convenience.

Addressing Modern Challenges

The frustrations many face in relationships today are often the result of misaligned expectations and a lack of spiritual grounding. The pervasive influence of secular dating norms, characterized by immediate gratification and a lack of accountability, has left many disillusioned and heartbroken. As believers, we are called to a higher standard, one that recognizes the sacredness of relationships and seeks to honor God in our interactions.

This guide will provide practical strategies for navigating the complexities of modern relationships while staying true to biblical principles. From understanding the importance of being equally yoked to developing communication skills that foster mutual respect and understanding, "Courting in the Kingdom" will equip you with the tools needed to build a relationship that stands the test of time.

Setting the Foundation

Before delving into the practical aspects of courtship, it is crucial to establish a strong spiritual foundation. This begins with a personal relationship with God, grounded in prayer and Scripture. As we seek His guidance and wisdom, we must also be willing to submit to His timing and plan for our lives.

In the chapters that follow, we will explore:

- **The Biblical Basis for Courtship:** Understanding the scriptural principles that underpin godly relationships.
- **Self-Preparation:** Developing the character and qualities necessary to be a godly partner.
- **Navigating Relationships:** Practical advice for establishing boundaries, fostering communication, and maintaining purity.
- **Discernment and Decision-Making:** Seeking God's will in choosing a life partner.

"Courting in the Kingdom: 10 Steps to Discern Your Perfect Match " is not just about finding a spouse; it is about transforming your approach to relationships to reflect the love and commitment that Christ has for His Church. As we embark on this journey together, may we be guided by the wisdom of Scripture, the leading of the Holy Spirit, and the example of Christ's sacrificial love.

Step 1: Seek God First

The Foundation of All Relationships

In the quest for a godly relationship, the starting point is not another person but rather our personal relationship with God. Matthew 6:33 provides a clear directive: "Seek first the kingdom of God and His righteousness, and all these things shall be added to you." This verse is not merely a guideline but a profound truth that underscores the importance of prioritizing our spiritual growth and relationship with God above all else, including our desire for a spouse.

Developing a Strong Personal Relationship with God

A strong personal relationship with God is the cornerstone of a fulfilling life and a prerequisite for a godly courtship. This relationship is cultivated through regular prayer, studying the Bible, and living out the principles found in Scripture. As we seek God daily, our hearts and minds are transformed, aligning our desires with His will.

Prayer: Prayer is our direct line of communication with God. It is through prayer that we pour out our hearts, seek His guidance, and listen for His voice. Consistent, heartfelt prayer builds intimacy with God, helping us to discern His will for every aspect of our lives, including relationships.

Bible Study: The Bible is God's revealed word to us, offering wisdom and guidance. Regularly reading and meditating on Scripture deepens our understanding of God's character and His design for our lives. Verses like Proverbs 3:5-6 remind us to trust in the Lord with all our hearts and acknowledge Him in all our ways, including our approach to relationships.

Worship and Community: Engaging in worship and being active in fellowship with a community of believers fosters spiritual growth and accountability. It is in the context of community that we receive encouragement, correction, and support from fellow believers, which is essential in our spiritual journey.

Finding Peace in Singleness

Before we can be ready for a relationship, we must be at peace with being single. This peace comes from understanding that our identity and worth are found in Christ, not in our relationship status. The apostle Paul, in Philippians 4:11-13, speaks of learning to be content in all circumstances. Contentment in singleness is a sign of spiritual maturity and readiness for the responsibilities of a relationship.

A true test of whether you are ready for a relationship is if you are at peace being single. This state of contentment indicates a whole and healthy mindset, showing that you do not need a relationship to feel complete. If, after a tough breakup, you feel the urge to quickly enter another relationship, it is a sign that you have not fully healed. Similarly, if you find yourself despising the idea of relationships, this also suggests unresolved hurt. The ideal balance lies in being content and at peace with your singleness while remaining open to and desiring a relationship. This equilibrium reflects a healthy readiness to embrace a new partnership grounded in wholeness and mutual respect.

Embrace Your Identity in Christ: Recognize that you are complete and whole in Christ. Colossians 2:10 declares, "And in Him, you have been made complete." This profound truth underscores that our true fulfillment and identity are found in our relationship with God, not in another person. Understanding this completeness means that we do not seek a partner to fill a void or make us whole; instead, we enter relationships from a place of fullness and strength. Our wholeness in Christ liberates us from the need for external validation, allowing us to approach relationships with a healthy perspective, rooted in God's unconditional love and purpose for our lives.

Find Purpose in Singleness: Use your season of singleness to serve God and others, maximizing this unique time to grow spiritually and make a meaningful impact. Engaging in ministry allows you to support those in need, reflecting Christ's love in practical ways. Developing your talents and pursuing your passions not only glorifies God but also brings personal fulfillment and joy. This period is an invaluable opportunity to deepen your faith, build your character, and cultivate skills that will enrich your future relationships and endeavors. Embrace this stage of life with purpose and enthusiasm, knowing that your efforts honor God and prepare you for the next chapter He has planned for you.

Seek Healing and Wholeness: Singleness is also a crucial time for personal growth and healing. It offers the opportunity to address past hurts and unresolved issues, allowing you to enter future relationships without the baggage of previous experiences. During this period, you can focus on developing healthy habits and routines that contribute to your overall well-being. Seeking emotional and spiritual wholeness during this time is essential, as it prepares you for a healthy, balanced relationship in the future. By investing in yourself and your personal growth now, you lay a strong foundation for a fulfilling and resilient partnership later on.

The Importance of Seeking the Kingdom First

Seeking the kingdom of God first means prioritizing our spiritual life and aligning our desires with God's will. When we seek God's kingdom, we trust that He will provide for our needs, including our desire for a spouse, in His perfect timing.

Align Your Desires with God's Will: As you grow in your relationship with God, your desires will begin to reflect His. Psalm 37:4 encourages us, "Delight yourself in the Lord, and He will give you the desires of your heart." This promise signifies that as we find joy and satisfaction in our relationship with God, our own desires will transform to align with His divine will. It doesn't mean that God will fulfill every personal wish, but rather that our hearts will start to desire what He desires for us. This alignment ensures that our goals and aspirations are in harmony with His perfect plan, leading to a more fulfilling and purposeful life.

Trust in God's Timing: Waiting for God's timing requires faith and patience, as it often challenges our desire for immediate answers and results. Proverbs 3:56 encourages us to "trust in the Lord with all your heart and lean not on your own understanding; in all your ways acknowledge Him, and He will make your paths straight." This verse reminds us that relying on God's wisdom, rather than our limited perspective, is essential. God's timing is perfect, and He orchestrates events in our lives with precision and purpose. Trusting in His plan means believing that He knows what is best for us, even when we cannot see the full picture. By exercising faith and patience, we align ourselves with His divine schedule, assured that His timing will bring about the best outcomes for our lives.

Focus on Spiritual Growth: Instead of fixating on finding a spouse, focus on growing spiritually. Prioritizing your relationship with God deepens your faith and enriches your character, preparing you for a future relationship. As you mature spiritually, you become more equipped to love, serve, and support a partner in a godly manner. Spiritual growth fosters qualities such as patience, kindness, and selflessness, which are essential for a healthy and thriving partnership. By dedicating this time to spiritual development, you align yourself with God's will and become a better version of yourself, ready to build a strong, Christ-centered relationship when the time is right.

Practical Steps for Seeking God First

To practically seek God first in your courtship process, consider implementing the following steps:

1. *Daily Devotions*: Set aside time each day for prayer and Bible study. Let these practices be the anchor of your day, grounding you in God's presence and wisdom.
2. *Regular Fasting*: Incorporate fasting into your spiritual routine. Fasting helps to sharpen your spiritual focus and align your desires with God's will.
3. *Active Participation in Fellowship*: Be actively involved in your church community. Join a small group, volunteer in ministries, and seek mentorship from mature believers.

4. *Journaling*: Keep a journal to record your prayers, reflections, and insights from your time with God. Journaling can help you track your spiritual growth and discern God's guidance in your life.

5. *Accountability Partners*: Choose trusted friends or mentors to hold you accountable in your spiritual journey. Share your struggles and victories with them, and seek their prayers and support.

God often sends us the kind of partner we have prepared ourselves for, mirroring the state of our own spiritual and emotional health. If we struggle with issues such as substance abuse or secretly watching pornography, it's likely that we will attract or be drawn to someone who also has similar afflictions. These unresolved issues create a spiritual and emotional resonance that pulls us towards partners who reflect our inner struggles. Therefore, it is crucial to address and heal these areas within ourselves, striving for holiness and purity.

The more we are able to heal ourselves and grow in holiness, the more we prepare ourselves for a pure and righteous partner. As we work on overcoming our personal challenges and aligning our lives with God's principles, we become more attuned to His will. This transformation allows us to attract a partner who shares our commitment to living a godly life. By becoming the best version of ourselves, we open the door to a relationship built on mutual respect, shared values, and spiritual growth, leading to a strong and fulfilling partnership that honors God.

By seeking God first and prioritizing your relationship with Him, you lay a solid foundation for a godly courtship. This approach not only prepares you for a future relationship but also enriches your life with peace, purpose, and a deep sense of fulfillment in Christ. As you seek His kingdom and righteousness, trust that God will lead you to the right person in His perfect timing.

Step 2: Understand the Marriage Blueprint

The Divine Design for Marriage

Marriage, as designed by God, is a sacred covenant reflecting His relationship with the Church. Ephesians 5:25-33 provides a clear picture of this divine blueprint, illustrating the roles of husband and wife and the profound mystery of two becoming one flesh.

Understanding this blueprint is essential for setting the right intentions in courtship and ensuring that our relationships honor God's design.

Setting Intentions for Righteous Courting

Worldly dating often prioritizes personal satisfaction, fleeting emotions, and superficial attractions. In contrast, righteous courting focuses on building a relationship that glorifies God, reflects His love, and lays a strong foundation for a lasting marriage. Here are the key elements of righteous courting:

Purpose-Driven: Courting is intentional and purposeful, aimed at discerning God's will for marriage, in stark contrast to the casual and often superficial nature of worldly dating. While dating in the secular world may prioritize immediate gratification, fun experiences, and exploring compatibility through a series of casual encounters, courting focuses on deepening emotional and spiritual connections with a long-term view. Courting emphasizes mutual respect, purity, and shared values, seeking to honor God throughout the relationship journey. It involves prayerful consideration, involvement of families and mentors, and intentional steps towards marriage readiness. Unlike worldly dating, which can be transient and self-centered, courting prioritizes the development of a committed and enduring partnership grounded in faith and mutual commitment to God's plan for marriage.

God-Centered: Every aspect of a God-centered relationship revolves around honoring God and aligning with His principles. Prayer, Bible study, and seeking godly counsel are not just optional but integral to the process. Through prayer, couples seek divine guidance and wisdom, inviting God into their relationship to lead and bless their journey together. Regular Bible study deepens their understanding of God's word and His design for marriage, providing a solid foundation for making decisions that reflect biblical values. Seeking godly counsel from trusted mentors and spiritual leaders offers invaluable insights and accountability, ensuring that their relationship stays on course according to God's will. By prioritizing these practices, couples nurture a relationship that grows in spiritual maturity, unity, and readiness for a lifelong commitment rooted in faith.

Purity: Righteous courting upholds the principles of physical and emotional purity, valuing each person's dignity and honoring God's commandments concerning sexuality. It acknowledges that sexual intimacy is a sacred gift designed by God to be shared within the commitment of marriage alone. Therefore, during courting, couples prioritize building a deep emotional connection and spiritual unity while respecting boundaries that preserve purity. This approach fosters mutual respect, trust, and a foundation of trustworthiness. It reflects a commitment to honor God's design for intimacy and to prepare for a marriage that prioritizes fidelity and the sanctity of marital intimacy.

Community Involvement*:* In courting, the involvement of family, church, and mentors plays a crucial role in fostering accountability and support within the broader community of believers. Beyond mere attendance at services, the church is understood as the unified body of Christ, where individuals come together in faith and fellowship. Family members provide wisdom and guidance, offering perspectives shaped by love and experience. Church community offers a foundation of shared beliefs and values, providing encouragement, prayer, and collective spiritual growth. Mentors, often mature married people who have walked the path of faith and relationships, offer invaluable insights and accountability. Together, these relational networks strengthen the couple's commitment to honoring God in their courtship journey, ensuring they are supported and guided by the collective wisdom and prayers of their Christ centered faith.

The Roles of Husband and Wife

Understanding the biblical roles of husband and wife is crucial in setting the right intentions for courtship:

Husbands: According to Ephesians 5:25-28, husbands are called to emulate Christ's sacrificial love for the Church in their relationship with their wives. This sacrificial love is characterized by selflessness, nurturing care, and a protective attitude that prioritizes the needs and well-being of their wives above their own. It entails a commitment to support, encourage, and uplift their spouses spiritually, emotionally, and physically. Just as Christ gave Himself up for the Church, husbands are called to sacrificially give of themselves for the sake of their wives' flourishing and happiness.

In this context, the husband serves as the covering for his wife, similar to how Christ is the covering for the Church. Being the covering means that the husband takes on the responsibility of leading with humility and grace, ensuring the spiritual and emotional safety of his wife. He creates an atmosphere of love and mutual respect within the marriage, guiding and protecting his family with a Christ-like attitude. This biblical mandate sets a high standard for husbands, calling them to embody a nurturing and selfless leadership that fosters a strong, loving, and God-honoring relationship.

Wives: Wives are encouraged by Ephesians 5:22-24 to respect and support their husbands, recognizing their leadership role within the marriage. This respect is not rooted in subservience but in a mutual understanding of each spouse's complementary roles and responsibilities. It involves honoring the husband's leadership and decision-making while working together in mutual submission under the guidance of Christ. This biblical teaching emphasizes the importance of unity and cooperation within marriage, where both partners contribute to the relationship's strength and harmony through their unique roles and mutual respect.

For wives to truly respect and support their husbands, they must overcome their own insecurities and learn to trust their husband's leadership. This process involves a journey of personal growth and faith, where a wife learns to rely on her husband's guidance while also maintaining her own identity and strength. By embodying respect and support, wives uphold the biblical principle of mutual submission and contribute to a loving, God-honoring marriage. This dynamic fosters an environment where both spouses can flourish and grow together in faith, creating a partnership that is both strong and harmonious.

Being Equally Yoked

The concept of being equally yoked comes from 2 Corinthians 6:14, which advises believers not to be unequally yoked with unbelievers. This principle extends beyond marriage to any close partnership or relationship, emphasizing the importance of shared faith and values. In the context of marriage, being equally yoked means that both partners share a deep, committed faith in Christ and are aligned in their spiritual values and goals. This spiritual alignment fosters a stronger, more resilient relationship, as both partners are committed to growing in their faith and supporting each other's spiritual journey. It ensures that their life together is built on a foundation of mutual beliefs and a shared vision for their future.

If people rush too fast in courting, they may not accurately gauge whether they are equally yoked in all aspects. Courting with patience and intentionality allows both individuals to thoroughly understand each other's faith, values, and long-term goals. Rushing can lead to overlooking significant differences that could cause conflicts and challenges later in the marriage. Taking the time to discern whether both partners are truly aligned spiritually ensures a more harmonious and God-centered relationship. By carefully evaluating compatibility and ensuring that both partners are equally committed to their faith, couples can build a marriage that honors God and stands the test of time.

Shared Faith: Both partners should have a personal relationship with Jesus Christ, follow God's laws and commandments, and be actively growing in their faith to ensure a strong, spiritually aligned foundation for their relationship. This means each individual prioritizes their personal walk with God, engaging in regular prayer, Bible study, and worship. They strive to live according to biblical principles, allowing God's Word to guide their actions and decisions. By continuously growing in their faith, they support and encourage one another's spiritual development, creating a partnership rooted in mutual respect, love, and commitment to God's will. This spiritual harmony not only strengthens their bond but also equips them to navigate life's challenges together, fostering a marriage that honors God and reflects His love.

Common Values: Core beliefs and values regarding God, family, morality, and life's purpose should align to create a harmonious and unified relationship. When partners share the same foundational principles, they can make decisions together with a common understanding and vision. This alignment includes a shared belief in God and commitment to living out His teachings, similar views on the importance and dynamics of family, consistent moral standards, and a united sense of purpose in life. Such alignment fosters mutual respect and support, reduces conflicts arising from differing worldviews, and strengthens the partnership. By being on the same page about these essential aspects, couples can build a stable, resilient relationship that reflects their shared faith and values, providing a strong platform for their journey together.

Mutual Commitment: Both partners should be committed to living out biblical principles in their daily lives and in their relationship, ensuring that their actions and decisions consistently reflect their faith. This commitment involves applying the teachings of Scripture in how they treat each other, manage their resources, and interact with the world around them. It means embodying qualities such as love, patience, kindness, and forgiveness, as outlined in passages like 1 Corinthians 13 and Galatians 5:22-23. By prioritizing biblical values, they create an environment of mutual respect, trust, and spiritual growth. This dedication to living out God's Word not only strengthens their bond but also serves as a testament to others of a Christcentered relationship, inspiring those around them to seek the same spiritual integrity in their own lives.

The Importance of Being Equally Yoked

Being equally yoked ensures that the couple can support each other spiritually, make unified decisions based on God's Word, and raise children in a godly environment. It minimizes conflicts that arise from fundamentally different worldviews and promotes harmony and peace in the marriage.

Spiritual Support: A couple that is equally yoked can pray together, worship together, and encourage each other in their spiritual journeys, creating a deeply rooted spiritual bond. Praying together allows them to seek God's guidance and support as a unified front, fostering intimacy and understanding. Worshiping together in fellowship and at home strengthens their connection with God and each other, providing shared experiences of faith and devotion. By encouraging one another in their spiritual growth, they become each other's strongest allies, offering support, accountability, and inspiration. This spiritual partnership not only enhances their individual relationships with God but also solidifies their commitment to a Christ-centered marriage, enabling them to face life's challenges with a united, faith-filled perspective.

Unified Decisions: Shared beliefs and values enable couples to make decisions that honor God and reflect His wisdom, providing a solid foundation for a harmonious and purpose-driven relationship. When both partners hold the same convictions about their faith, morals, and life goals, they can navigate life's choices with a unified approach that aligns with biblical teachings. This common ground allows them to seek God's guidance together, ensuring their decisions are rooted in prayer and Scripture. It fosters mutual respect and understanding, reducing conflicts and enhancing cooperation. By consistently making decisions that reflect God's wisdom, they not only strengthen their bond but also set a powerful example for others, demonstrating the beauty and strength of a relationship built on shared spiritual values.

Godly Legacy: Raising children with consistent spiritual teachings and examples of godly living creates a strong foundation for the next generation, instilling values that endure beyond childhood. When parents model a life centered on faith, integrity, and compassion, they provide a framework for their children to understand and embrace biblical principles. This upbringing equips them to navigate life's challenges with wisdom and resilience, grounded in a deep understanding of God's love and purpose for their lives. Consistent spiritual guidance fosters a sense of security and identity rooted in faith, empowering children to make choices that honor God and positively impact their communities. Ultimately, the legacy of faith passed down through generations not only strengthens family bonds but also contributes to a broader culture of righteousness and hope.

Practical Steps to Ensure Being Equally Yoked

1. *Discuss Faith Early*: Early in the courtship, it is crucial to have open and honest conversations about your faith, beliefs, and spiritual practices. Ensure that you both understand the importance of faith in each other's lives and are genuinely aligned in your spiritual values. *Be truthful and authentic in these discussions, resisting the urge to change your views to impress or agree with the other person.* It is far better to be honest and discover early on whether you are truly compatible than to wear a mask and later realize that your differences make the relationship untenable. This honesty lays a foundation of trust and clarity, essential for building a strong, lasting partnership.

2. *Engage in Spiritual Activities Together*: Attend fellowship services, Bible studies, and prayer meetings together. Observe how each other lives out their faith in various aspects of life.

3. *Seek Counsel from Spiritual Mentors*: Involving pastors, mentors, and mature believers in your courtship can be invaluable. Their

insights and observations can help discern whether you and your partner are truly equally yoked. These individuals often have years of experience and wisdom in navigating relationships and can provide objective advice and guidance. They can help you see potential issues you might overlook and offer biblical counsel to ensure your relationship aligns with God's will. Their involvement adds a layer of accountability and support, helping you make wise decisions throughout the courtship process.

However, it is crucial to be mindful of who you take advice from, preferring insights from happily married individuals over single people. While single friends and mentors can offer valuable perspectives, they may lack the lived experience of maintaining a successful marriage. Married individuals, especially those in happy and godly unions, can speak from a place of authority and share practical, tested wisdom. Be cautious of advice from those who speak from their own places of failure, as their perspectives may be influenced by unresolved issues or disappointments. Surrounding yourself with godly, experienced counsel will provide a balanced and informed view, enhancing your discernment in choosing a lifelong partner.

4. *Pray for Discernment*: Regularly pray for God's guidance and wisdom in your relationship. Ask Him to reveal any areas of concern and to strengthen your bond in Christ.

Embracing the Biblical Blueprint

Embracing the biblical blueprint for marriage requires a commitment to God's design and principles. By setting intentions for righteous courting rather than worldly dating, we align our relationships with His will and prepare for a marriage that honors Him. Understanding and applying the concept of being equally yoked ensures that we build a partnership grounded in shared faith and values.

As we seek to follow God's blueprint for marriage, let us remember that the ultimate goal is to reflect His love and glory in our relationships. By prioritizing spiritual growth, maintaining purity, and involving the Church community, we lay a foundation for a marriage that is not only fulfilling but also a powerful testimony of God's grace and love to the world.

Step 3: Develop Personal Character

We attract what we are, a principle that highlights the importance of personal character development in the pursuit of meaningful relationships. Often, individuals with outward or hidden character defects unknowingly attract others with similar flaws, leading to relationships fraught with conflict and dissatisfaction. It's a common pitfall to believe oneself better than the people they attract, failing to recognize that their own undeveloped traits are the magnet drawing in such partners. By acknowledging and addressing these character flaws, individuals can break this cycle, leading to healthier and more fulfilling relationships.

Developing personal character is crucial for attracting partners with a higher quality of character. As individuals grow in integrity, humility, forgiveness, and other godly attributes, they naturally become more confident in identifying and weeding out those who do not meet their standards. This heightened discernment is invaluable in the courting process, ensuring that relationships are built on a solid foundation of shared values and mutual respect. Furthermore, individuals who have invested in their personal growth are better prepared for the challenges of marriage, equipped with the virtues necessary to build a lasting, Christ-centered union. This proactive approach to character development not only enhances personal well-being but also paves the way for a fulfilling and Godhonoring marriage.

Cultivating the Fruits of the Spirit

In the journey towards a godly relationship, developing personal character and spiritual maturity is paramount. Galatians 5:22-23 identifies the fruits of the Spirit—love, joy, peace, patience, kindness, goodness, faithfulness, gentleness, and self-control—as foundational virtues to cultivate in one's life. These qualities are not just admirable traits but essential aspects of a Christ-like character that attracts and sustains a godly partnership.

Embracing Love

Love, as delineated in Galatians 5:22-23, serves as the bedrock of Christ like faith and relationships, embodying qualities of selflessness and sacrificial care. Modeled after God's unconditional love for humanity, epitomized through Christ's sacrifice, genuine love in relationships transcends superficial emotions. It entails a commitment to prioritize the well-being and growth of the other person, manifesting in acts of kindness, patience, and forgiveness. This sacrificial love cultivates trust and intimacy, creating a foundation where both partners can navigate life's challenges together with grace and empathy. By embodying these qualities, couples not only strengthen their bond but also exemplify God's love in their relationship, reflecting His grace and compassion to those around them.

Love in Christ like relationships extend beyond passionate feelings to encompass a profound commitment to honor God and serve one another. It fosters a deep sense of unity and mutual respect, where each partner seeks to uplift and support the other in their journey of faith. This love is characterized by humility and selflessness, mirroring Christ's example of servant leadership. It compels couples to prioritize spiritual growth and encourage each other's pursuit of God's will. Through prayer, shared devotionals, and mutual accountability, they nurture a relationship that glorifies God and embodies His principles of love and grace.

As couples embrace God's definition of love, they experience transformation both individually and collectively. Love as described in Galatians 5:22-23 prompts couples to cultivate a lifestyle of compassion, patience, and understanding. It inspires them to extend grace and forgiveness, mirroring God's boundless mercy toward humanity. This love empowers couples to navigate challenges with resilience and faith, knowing that their relationship is anchored in God's steadfast love. By continually seeking to embody the fruits of the Spirit, couples not only strengthen their bond but also become beacons of God's love in a world in need of hope and reconciliation.

Experiencing Joy

Joy, one of the fruits of the Spirit mentioned in Galatians 5:22-23, plays a transformative role in nurturing healthy and thriving relationships. Unlike fleeting happiness dependent on external circumstances, joy in the context of relationships is rooted in a deep-seated contentment and gratitude that stems from faith in God. This joy enables couples to find fulfillment and satisfaction in God's presence and promises, irrespective of the challenges they face together. It becomes a steadfast source of strength and resilience, allowing partners to navigate difficulties with positivity and hope.

In relationships, joy fosters an atmosphere of celebration and thankfulness, where every moment shared is viewed as a gift from God. It encourages couples to appreciate and cherish one another, creating a sense of warmth and closeness that deepens their bond. Joy also serves as a counterbalance to stress and adversity, helping couples to maintain perspective and respond to challenges with grace and optimism. By cultivating joy, couples not only enhance their own emotional well-being but also uplift and inspire each other, reinforcing a positive and supportive partnership.

Furthermore, joy in relationships extends beyond individual feelings to become a shared experience that strengthens unity and mutual understanding. It fosters a sense of camaraderie and partnership, where couples rejoice in each other's successes and find solace in God's presence during times of difficulty. This communal joy enriches communication and fosters a spirit of collaboration, encouraging couples to face life's journey together with resilience and faith. Ultimately, joy as a fruit of the Spirit enriches relationships by infusing them with gratitude, positivity, and a deep appreciation for the blessings of God in their lives.

Pursuing Peace and Patience

Pursuing peace and patience in relationships is essential for fostering resilience, understanding, and growth. Peace, as described in Galatians 5:22-23, goes beyond mere absence of conflict; it embodies a deep-seated tranquility rooted in faith and trust in God's sovereignty and grace. This inner peace enables couples to navigate life's uncertainties with a sense of calm and assurance, knowing that God is in control. By cultivating peace within themselves and their relationship, couples create a harmonious environment where communication flows freely, misunderstandings are resolved peacefully, and unity is strengthened.

Patience, closely intertwined with peace, plays a vital role in nurturing healthy relationships. It involves steadfast endurance and forbearance during challenging times, allowing individuals to grow personally and as a couple. Patience fosters empathy and understanding, as partners learn to appreciate each other's strengths and weaknesses over time. It teaches couples to wait on God's timing and guidance, rather than rushing decisions or becoming discouraged by setbacks.

Through practicing patience, couples develop resilience and deepen their commitment to each other, building a foundation of trust and mutual support that sustains their relationship through life's ups and downs.

Together, peace and patience create a framework for lasting harmony and growth in relationships. They encourage couples to approach challenges with grace and humility, seeking reconciliation and understanding rather than conflict or impatience. By prioritizing these fruits of the Spirit, couples honor God's desire for unity and mutual respect in relationships. They lay a foundation where love flourishes, communication thrives, and faith in God's providence remains steadfast. In embracing peace and patience, couples not only strengthen their bond but also exemplify God's transformative power in their lives and relationships.

Practicing Kindness and Goodness

Practicing kindness and goodness in relationships cultivates an atmosphere of compassion, integrity, and mutual respect. Kindness, as highlighted in Galatians 5:22-23, involves genuine empathy and consideration for others' well-being. In relationships, kindness is demonstrated through thoughtful actions, words of encouragement, and gestures of support that uplift and strengthen one's partner. It fosters a culture of care and understanding, where each person feels valued and cherished. By prioritizing kindness, couples create a nurturing environment where love can flourish and grow.

Goodness, closely related to kindness, embodies moral excellence and uprightness in every aspect of life. It is about consistently choosing what is right and honorable, even in challenging circumstances. In relationships, goodness manifests through honesty, loyalty, and a commitment to ethical behavior. Couples who practice goodness prioritize integrity and trustworthiness, laying a foundation of mutual respect and transparency. This moral compass guides their decisions and interactions, ensuring that their relationship reflects God's principles of righteousness and grace.

Together, kindness and goodness form pillars of strength and virtue in relationships. They inspire couples to treat each other with dignity and grace, fostering a deep sense of connection and mutual support. By embracing these fruits of the Spirit, couples not only enhance their own character but also contribute positively to their relationship's growth and stability. Kindness and goodness create a harmonious partnership where love is expressed through selfless actions and moral integrity, reflecting God's love and wisdom in every aspect of their lives together.

Committing to Faithfulness and Gentleness

Committing to faithfulness and gentleness in relationships establishes a foundation of trust, respect, and emotional security. Faithfulness, as emphasized in Galatians 5:22-23, signifies unwavering loyalty and reliability in honoring commitments. In a romantic context, it involves steadfast dedication to one's partner, demonstrating trustworthiness and consistency in words and actions. Just as God remains faithful to His promises, couples who prioritize faithfulness cultivate a deep sense of security and mutual respect in their relationship. This commitment to fidelity nurtures a bond built on trust and strengthens the emotional connection between partners.

Gentleness, often misconstrued as weakness, embodies a strength of character characterized by humility, empathy, and sensitivity towards others. In relationships, gentleness fosters a climate of understanding and compassion, where partners communicate with kindness and respect. It involves listening attentively, speaking with grace, and responding to conflicts or challenges with patience and empathy. This gentle approach allows couples to navigate disagreements constructively, prioritizing harmony and mutual growth. By practicing gentleness, couples cultivate an environment where love flourishes and where each partner feels valued and cherished for who they are.

Together, faithfulness and gentleness contribute to the development of a healthy and thriving relationship rooted in mutual respect and care. These fruits of the Spirit enable couples to build a partnership characterized by trust, emotional intimacy, and shared values. By committing to faithfulness, couples honor their commitment to each other and to God, fostering a relationship where loyalty and reliability are valued virtues. Simultaneously, embracing gentleness fosters an atmosphere of grace and understanding, ensuring that conflicts are resolved with humility and compassion. Ultimately, by embodying these qualities, couples reflect God's love and grace in their relationship, creating a lasting and meaningful union centered on mutual respect and steadfast devotion.

Exercising Self-Control

Exercising self-control, the final fruit of the Spirit mentioned in Galatians 5:22-23, plays a crucial role in fostering healthy relationships grounded in wisdom and righteousness. Self-control involves the ability to manage one's desires, impulses, and actions in alignment with God's will and moral principles. In the context of relationships, self-control enables individuals to refrain from impulsive reactions or decisions that could harm themselves or their partner. It promotes thoughtful and deliberate choices that prioritize the well-being of both parties and honor God's standards of integrity and respect.

Self-control fosters discipline and maturity in individuals, cultivating a foundation of trust and reliability within the relationship. By exercising selfcontrol, couples demonstrate their commitment to upholding values such as fidelity, honesty, and mutual respect. This virtue empowers partners to navigate challenges and temptations with resilience and grace, ensuring that their interactions are characterized by wisdom and discernment. In moments of conflict or uncertainty, self-control allows individuals to respond with patience and empathy, promoting understanding and reconciliation rather than escalation.

In embracing self-control, couples create an environment where mutual trust and emotional safety thrive. They uphold a standard of behavior that reflects God's righteousness and encourages personal growth. By consistently exercising self-control, individuals contribute to the strength and stability of their relationship, fostering a climate of harmony and mutual support. This intentional practice not only enhances individual character but also strengthens the partnership, paving the way for a relationship founded on faith, integrity, and enduring love.

Avoid Self Pleasure

Masturbation and pornography are prevalent temptations in today's society, often seen as harmless ways for single individuals to cope with sexual desires. However, indulging in these behaviors can significantly diminish the passion and drive necessary for meaningful courtship, reducing the excitement and commitment that build strong relationships. The Bible advises us to flee from lust, as stated in 1 Corinthians 6:18, "Flee from sexual immorality. Every other sin a person commits is outside the body, but the sexually immoral person sins against his own body." This wisdom underscores the importance of maintaining sexual purity and channeling those energies into wholesome pursuits that honor God.

Additionally, the act of masturbation can foster a sense of complacency, causing individuals to become more content with themselves and less motivated to seek genuine, fulfilling partnerships. This behavior often serves as a gateway to pornography, a habit that not only damages personal integrity but also supports an industry rooted in exploitation and degradation. Genesis 38:9-10 illustrates the seriousness of wasting one's seed, as Onan's actions displeased the Lord. By succumbing to these urges, individuals invite negative spiritual influences into their lives and develop unrealistic expectations for sexual relationships, which can lead to disappointment and strife in marriage.

To guard against these pitfalls, it is crucial to keep one's mind focused on holiness and righteousness. In a world saturated with sexual imagery and permissive attitudes, striving to avoid entertainment that promotes such content is essential. Philippians 4:8 encourages believers to dwell on whatever is true, honorable, just, pure, lovely, and commendable. While nobody is perfect, pursuing the highest ideals of purity and respect in relationships is vital for spiritual health and personal growth. By avoiding masturbation and pornography, individuals can foster deeper connections and live in alignment with God's will for their lives. Know in your heart that you can do it. If you slip, don't beat yourself up. Dust yourself off and strive again. It will be challenging, fervent praying for a pure mind in Christ will be necessary

Additional Godly Character Attributes

Humility: Humility involves recognizing one's limitations and dependence on God, acknowledging that our abilities and successes are gifts from Him. This recognition fosters a deep sense of gratitude and prevents the development of pride and arrogance. When we understand that our strengths and achievements are not solely the result of our efforts but are blessings from God, we become more reliant on His guidance and grace. This dependence on God cultivates a spirit of humility, reminding us that we are not self-sufficient and need His wisdom and strength in every aspect of our lives.

Moreover, humility is about valuing others above oneself and treating them with respect and kindness. It means putting the needs and well-being of others before our own, reflecting the selfless love that Jesus demonstrated. By avoiding pride and arrogance, we create an environment where others feel valued and respected, fostering stronger and more meaningful relationships. Humility allows us to listen to others, learn from them, and appreciate their contributions. It also encourages us to admit our mistakes and seek forgiveness, promoting a culture of mutual respect and growth. In essence, humility is a cornerstone of godly character that enhances our relationships with God and others, creating a more compassionate and connected community.

Forgiveness: Forgiveness is a fundamental aspect of Christ like character, rooted in the willingness to forgive others as God has forgiven us. This act of forgiveness requires us to let go of grudges and bitterness, which can otherwise fester and damage our relationships and personal well-being. By forgiving others, we acknowledge the grace that God has extended to us and extend that same grace to those who have wronged us. This process is not always easy, but it is essential for maintaining a healthy spiritual life and fostering an environment of love and understanding.

Promoting reconciliation and healing through forgiveness is vital for personal and communal growth. When we forgive, we pave the way for mending broken relationships and restoring harmony. This act of grace not only heals the one who has been wronged but also liberates the one who forgives, freeing them from the burden of resentment. Forgiveness is a powerful testimony of God's love and mercy, demonstrating the transformative power of His grace in our lives. By embodying forgiveness, we contribute to a more compassionate and unified community, reflecting the heart of Christ in our interactions with others.

Integrity: Integrity involves maintaining consistency in moral and ethical principles, ensuring that our actions align with our beliefs and values in all aspects of life. It means being honest and trustworthy, even when it is challenging or inconvenient. A person of integrity does not compromise their principles for personal gain or convenience; instead, they uphold the truth and strive to do what is right, regardless of the circumstances. This steadfast commitment to ethical behavior fosters trust and respect from others, as they can rely on the person's word and actions to be consistent and dependable.

Reflecting God's truthfulness, integrity is a vital component of a godly character. God is inherently truthful and faithful, and as His followers, we are called to emulate these attributes. By being truthful and faithful in our own lives, we demonstrate the transformative power of God's truth and grace. Integrity also builds a solid foundation for all relationships, as trust is crucial for genuine connection and mutual respect. When we live with integrity, we not only honor God but also create a positive influence in our communities, encouraging others to pursue righteousness and ethical living.

Attracting a Godly Partner

Attracting a godly partner begins with cultivating the fruits of the Spirit—love, joy, peace, patience, kindness, goodness, faithfulness, gentleness, and self-control—in one's own life. These qualities reflect a commitment to personal growth and spiritual maturity, making an individual more attractive to someone who values godliness and seeks a Christ-centered relationship. A godly character is magnetic, drawing those who share similar values and aspirations in honoring God through their relationships. This foundation of spiritual alignment fosters mutual respect, understanding, and harmony from the outset, laying a strong groundwork for a partnership rooted in faith and mutual edification.

A commitment to developing these fruits of the Spirit not only enhances personal character but also enriches one's interactions and relationships. It demonstrates a genuine desire to live out biblical principles and values, which resonates deeply with a potential partner who prioritizes faith and spiritual growth. Individuals who exemplify these qualities not only attract like-minded individuals but also contribute positively to the health and longevity of their relationships. This intentional focus on spiritual development creates a relational environment where both partners can support and encourage each other's journey of faith, fostering a deep connection and shared commitment to God's plan for their lives together.

Moreover, a godly character rooted in the fruits of the Spirit serves as a testimony of God's transformative power and grace. It reflects a heart that seeks to glorify God in all aspects of life, including relationships. This authenticity and sincerity draw others who are also seeking to live out their faith with integrity and purpose. By embodying these qualities, individuals not only position themselves to attract a godly partner but also contribute to building a Christ-centered relationship founded on mutual trust, spiritual compatibility, and a shared vision for honoring God in their lives together.

Step 4: Pray for Guidance

Prayer is foundational to the journey of seeking a spouse in alignment with God's will. James 1:5 encourages believers to seek wisdom from God, who generously provides without reproach. This verse underscores the importance of prayer in discerning God's guidance in every aspect of life, including relationships. Consistently praying for wisdom and discernment in choosing a spouse invites God into the process, acknowledging His sovereignty and wisdom above our own.

Prayer serves as a direct line of communication with God, allowing individuals to present their desires, concerns, and uncertainties before Him. By seeking His guidance through prayer, individuals demonstrate trust in His plan and timing. This reliance on God's wisdom helps navigate the complexities of relationships with clarity and confidence, ensuring that decisions are rooted in His perfect will rather than personal desires or societal pressures.

Furthermore, prayer for guidance fosters spiritual growth and sensitivity to God's voice. It invites individuals to align their hearts with His purposes, seeking a partner who shares their commitment to faith and values. Through prayer, individuals gain insight into the character and intentions of potential partners, discerning whether their relationship aligns with God's principles of love, respect, and mutual support. Ultimately, praying for guidance in choosing a spouse is an act of faith that invites God to lead and direct, ensuring that His blessings and favor accompany the journey toward a God-honoring marriage.

Here are some ways to pray for wisdom and discernment:

Seeking God's Guidance

Seeking God's guidance is foundational to making wise decisions, especially when it comes to matters as significant as choosing a spouse. Acknowledging God's sovereignty and wisdom is the first step in this journey. Recognizing that God has a perfect plan for our lives and relationships allows us to approach Him with humility and trust. By acknowledging His sovereignty, we affirm our belief that He knows what is best for us and that His plans are far greater than our own.

Praying for clarity in understanding God's will is essential. This involves seeking His wisdom and insight into the specific direction He has for our lives, including our relationships. Clarity in discerning God's will enables us to make informed decisions that align with His purposes and values. It involves surrendering our desires and expectations to Him, trusting that He will guide us toward a path that leads to His blessings and fulfillment.

Discernment plays a crucial role in seeking God's guidance. It requires us to actively listen to His voice through prayer, meditation on His Word, and seeking counsel from wise mentors and trusted advisors. Discernment helps us distinguish between God's leading and our own desires or external pressures. It empowers us to make choices that honor God and contribute to our spiritual growth and well-being. Seeking God's guidance through prayer and discernment sets a firm foundation for navigating the complexities of relationships with faith, wisdom, and confidence in His providence.

Specific Requests

Being specific in prayer is crucial when seeking God's guidance in relationships, particularly in the search for a life partner. It involves articulating your desires, concerns, and uncertainties before God with clarity and sincerity. Asking God to reveal His plan for your relationships invites His guidance and direction into the process. This specificity demonstrates trust in His wisdom and timing, believing that He knows the desires of your heart and will lead you accordingly.

Praying for wisdom in evaluating potential partners is another vital aspect of specific requests. This includes asking God to grant discernment in assessing character, values, and compatibility with His purposes. Wisdom in this context extends beyond mere attraction or superficial qualities, encompassing a deeper understanding of how a potential partner aligns with God's principles and your personal values. Through specific prayers, you seek clarity on whether a relationship is God-honoring and conducive to mutual growth in faith and love.

Moreover, specific requests in prayer foster a deeper intimacy with God as you share your hopes and concerns with Him. It creates a dialogue where you actively seek His guidance and involve Him in every aspect of your relationship journey. By being specific in your prayers, you demonstrate dependence on God's wisdom and trust in His provision, believing that He will lead you to a partner who complements your spiritual journey and shares your commitment to honoring Him in all things.

Openness to God's Voice

Openness to God's voice is essential in discerning His will and guidance in relationships. This involves praying earnestly for a receptive heart and a keen sensitivity to God's leading through various channels. By seeking openness in prayer, individuals invite God to speak to them directly through His Word, which serves as a timeless source of wisdom and truth. It is through Scripture that God reveals His character, His plans, and His principles for relationships, guiding individuals in making decisions that align with His divine purposes.

In addition to Scripture, openness to God's voice includes prayer as a means of intimate communication with Him. Through prayer, individuals not only express their desires and concerns but also listen attentively for God's responses and nudges. This dialogue with God fosters a deeper relationship and builds trust in His guidance. Moreover, seeking counsel from wise mentors and trusted advisors is instrumental in being open to God's voice. These individuals can provide spiritual insight, practical wisdom, and discernment from their own experiences and understanding of God's Word, offering perspectives that help clarify and confirm God's direction in relationships.

Being open to God's voice through His Word, prayer, and wise counsel creates a holistic approach to seeking His guidance in relationships. It requires humility to listen and discern His leading, trusting that His plans surpass our own understanding. This openness cultivates a posture of faith and obedience, where individuals actively seek God's wisdom and submit to His will, confident that He will direct their paths toward relationships that honor Him and fulfill His purposes.

Discernment of Character

 Praying for discernment in assessing the character, values, and intentions of potential partners is crucial in making wise relationship decisions. It involves seeking God's guidance to perceive beyond outward appearances and initial impressions, delving deeper into the heart and motivations of individuals. By praying for discernment, individuals ask God to grant them insight into the true character and integrity of potential partners, helping to distinguish genuine qualities from superficial traits.

Asking God to help see beyond external appearances aligns with His desire for relationships based on sincerity and mutual respect. It encourages individuals to look for qualities that reflect God's values and principles, such as honesty, humility, and a commitment to righteousness. Through prayer, individuals invite God to reveal whether a potential partner's values and aspirations align with His purposes, ensuring that relationships are founded on shared faith and mutual understanding. This prayerful approach to discernment fosters clarity and confidence in navigating the complexities of relationships, seeking God's guidance every step of the way.

Strength in Decision-Making

Strength in decision-making is crucial when navigating relationships, especially when seeking God's will for a life partner. It involves praying for the fortitude and courage to align decisions with God's plan, even if they go against popular opinion or personal desires. By seeking God's strength through prayer, individuals find assurance and resilience to make choices that honor Him, prioritizing His guidance above all else. This reliance on God's strength empowers individuals to remain steadfast in their convictions, trusting that His wisdom surpasses human understanding.

Having confidence in decisions made through prayer and discernment is essential for maintaining faith and clarity in relationships. Confidence stems from trusting God's promises and knowing that His plans are for our welfare and not harm, to give us a future and a hope. This assurance enables individuals to navigate uncertainties with grace and perseverance, knowing that their decisions are rooted in seeking God's best for their lives and relationships.

Furthermore, strength in decision-making through prayer cultivates a deeper reliance on God's guidance and provision. It reinforces the belief that God equips His followers with the courage and resilience needed to uphold His principles and follow His leading. This steadfastness in faith and decision-making fosters a relationship built on trust and obedience, where individuals can confidently pursue relationships that align with God's purpose and bring fulfillment to their lives.

Patience and Trust

Patience and trust are indispensable virtues when seeking God's will in relationships, as they emphasize reliance on His timing and wisdom. Praying for patience involves surrendering personal timelines and desires to God, acknowledging His sovereignty over the course of our lives. It entails asking for the grace to wait with faith and endurance, knowing that God's timing is always perfect and His plans are designed for our ultimate good. Through prayer, individuals seek the strength to remain steadfast in their trust in God, even when faced with uncertainty or longing for answers.

Trusting in God's timing is essential for maintaining hope and peace during seasons of waiting. It requires believing that He orchestrates every detail of our lives with purpose and care, including our relationships. By entrusting our desires and uncertainties to Him in prayer, we affirm our faith that He will guide us toward fulfilling His plans in His perfect time. Trusting in God's timing also fosters a deeper intimacy with Him, as we learn to rely on His faithfulness and provision throughout the journey of seeking a life partner.

Moreover, patience and trust in God's timing cultivate resilience and maturity in relationships. They enable individuals to approach potential partners with a balanced perspective, free from impatience or anxiety. By praying for patience and trusting in God's timing, individuals embrace a posture of surrender and readiness to embrace His plans, knowing that He will lead them to the right person at the appointed time. This reliance on God's guidance not only strengthens their faith but also deepens their relationship with Him, fostering a journey of growth and spiritual fulfillment.

Protection from Harm

Praying for protection from relationships that may lead us away from God's purposes or cause harm to our spiritual and emotional well-being is crucial for maintaining a healthy and God-honoring journey in seeking a life partner. This prayer acknowledges our vulnerability to relationships that may distract us from our faith or compromise our values. By asking God for protection, we seek His guidance in discerning potential pitfalls and avoiding connections that could hinder our spiritual growth or lead us astray.

Protection in prayer encompasses safeguarding our hearts and minds from relationships that do not align with God's plan for our lives. It involves asking God to shield us from emotional entanglements or influences that may cloud our judgment or diminish our commitment to Him. Through prayer, we entrust our relational pursuits to God, seeking His wisdom and discernment to recognize red flags and make decisions that reflect His truth and love.

Furthermore, praying for protection invites God to intervene and guide us toward relationships that are rooted in His principles of love, respect, and mutual edification. It reinforces our dependence on His strength and discernment, affirming our faith that He is faithful to guard our hearts and direct our paths. By prioritizing protection in prayer, individuals cultivate a mindset of vigilance and discernment, ensuring that their relational choices honor God and contribute to their spiritual wellbeing.

Gratitude and Surrender

Ending prayers with gratitude and surrender is a powerful way to affirm our trust in God's faithfulness and sovereignty over our lives, including our journey to find a life partner. Expressing gratitude acknowledges God's past provisions, answered prayers, and continual presence in our lives. It cultivates a heart of thankfulness for His guidance thus far and instills confidence that He will continue to lead us in His perfect timing. Surrendering to His guidance involves relinquishing our own plans and desires to align with His will, recognizing that His ways are higher and His thoughts are greater than ours.

By ending prayers with gratitude and surrender, individuals cultivate a posture of humility and dependence on God. This practice deepens our relationship with Him as we acknowledge His wisdom and goodness in every aspect of our lives, including relationships. It encourages a mindset of trust and expectancy, knowing that God's blessings are abundant and His timing is always perfect. Surrendering our desires and plans to Him in prayer allows us to walk confidently in His guidance, confident that He will lead us toward relationships that honor Him and bring fulfillment to our lives.

The Importance of Prayer

By consistently praying for wisdom and discernment in the process of choosing a spouse, individuals actively invite God to participate in this significant decision. This ongoing prayerful approach reflects a deep desire to seek God's will and align one's choices with His divine plan. It demonstrates a commitment to placing God at the center of the relationship journey, trusting His wisdom and guidance above personal preferences or societal pressures. Through prayer, individuals acknowledge their dependence on God's direction, believing that He knows the desires of their heart and will lead them toward a partnership that glorifies Him and contributes to their spiritual growth.

Seeking God's direction through prayer fosters a relationship rooted in faith and obedience. It instills a sense of peace and confidence that God's plan is unfolding according to His perfect timing and purposes. By relying on His wisdom, individuals navigate the complexities of relationships with clarity and discernment, ensuring that their choices honor God and align with His values. Consistent prayer for wisdom and discernment not only invites God into the decisionmaking process but also strengthens the foundation of trust and reliance on His guidance, paving the way for a fulfilling and God-honoring relationship journey.

Step 5: Know Yourself and Your Purpose

Knowing yourself and your purpose is crucial in a Godcentered marriage for several reasons. Knowing yourself profoundly impacts various aspects of marriage, starting with communication and emotional regulation. When you have a clear understanding of your own emotions, needs, and triggers, you can communicate more effectively with your spouse. This self-awareness allows you to express your thoughts and feelings honestly and constructively, facilitating open and transparent dialogue. By recognizing your own emotional responses, you can manage them better during conflicts, reducing the likelihood of overreacting or misinterpreting your partner's actions. This emotional regulation helps maintain a calm and supportive environment, essential for resolving disagreements and nurturing a healthy relationship.

Furthermore, knowing yourself enhances intimacy and personal growth within the marriage. When you understand your desires, preferences, and vulnerabilities, you can share these with your spouse, fostering a deeper emotional and physical connection. This transparency builds trust and strengthens the bond between partners. Additionally, self-awareness encourages personal development, allowing you to bring your best self to the relationship. As you work on your strengths and address areas for improvement, you contribute positively to the marriage, promoting mutual growth and a more fulfilling partnership. Understanding yourself also helps align your life goals and values with those of your spouse, ensuring you both work towards common objectives and a shared vision for your future together.

Understanding your God-given purpose provides direction and meaning to your marriage. When both partners are clear about their individual and collective callings, they can align their goals and efforts towards fulfilling God's will. This shared sense of purpose enhances the spiritual depth of the relationship, ensuring that decisions and actions are guided by a higher calling. It helps the couple stay focused on their divine mission, navigating life's challenges with a clear sense of direction and unity. A God-centered marriage thrives when both individuals are rooted in their identity and purpose, working together to glorify God in all aspects of their lives.

The Importance of Self Awareness

Self-awareness starts with an honest assessment of who you are. It allows you to understand your strengths, weaknesses, and areas needing growth, which is essential for fostering a healthy and honest relationship with your spouse. By recognizing your strengths, you can contribute positively to the relationship and use these attributes to support your partner. Acknowledging your weaknesses and areas needing growth helps in maintaining humility and a willingness to improve, which is crucial for resolving conflicts and fostering mutual respect. When both partners are committed to personal growth, they create a dynamic where both individuals are continually evolving, enriching the relationship.

Knowing your triggers and vulnerabilities is also a significant aspect of self-awareness. These can stem from past experiences, personality traits passed down from your upbringing, and the character of your parents. Understanding how these factors influence your behavior allows you to navigate your reactions more effectively and communicate them to your spouse. For instance, if certain actions or words trigger negative emotions due to past experiences, being aware of this helps you to address the root cause rather than projecting it onto your partner. This level of understanding promotes a deeper emotional connection and trust within the relationship.

Furthermore, self-awareness involves recognizing the impact of past relationships and your environment on your current self. Reflecting on how previous relationships have shaped your expectations, fears, and desires allows you to break unhealthy patterns and foster a healthier dynamic in your marriage. Similarly, understanding how your environment has influenced your worldview and behavior helps you to stand stronger in relation to your partner. The more self-aware you are, the better you can support each other's growth, working together more effectively and creating a strong, unified partnership. This foundation of mutual understanding and respect is crucial for a thriving, Godcentered marriage.

Self-awareness leads to vulnerability and transparency, key components of intimacy in marriage. When you know yourself, you can communicate your needs, desires, and concerns more effectively with your spouse. This level of communication fosters trust and deepens the emotional connection between partners. It also means being open to feedback and willing to change for the betterment of the relationship. A marriage where both partners are committed to selfawareness and personal growth is one where mutual respect and understanding thrive, paving the way for a resilient and loving partnership.

Presenting Your Authentic Self

Authenticity in matrimony begins with knowing yourself, which allows you to present your true self to your partner. When you understand your values, desires, and insecurities, you can communicate them honestly, fostering a relationship built on genuine understanding. This authenticity creates an environment where both partners feel safe to express their true selves without fear of judgment or rejection. Being open and honest about who you are helps establish a foundation of trust, as there are no hidden facets or pretenses to create misunderstandings or conflicts.

This level of authenticity deepens the connection between partners, as it encourages a more profound and meaningful interaction. When both individuals are true to themselves and each other, they can support each other's growth and navigate challenges with a united front. This mutual acceptance strengthens the emotional bond, promoting a sense of security and intimacy. Authenticity also enhances mutual respect, as both partners appreciate and value each other for who they truly are, rather than who they think they should be. By embracing authenticity, couples can cultivate a relationship marked by trust, respect, and a deep, enduring connection.

Setting Healthy Boundaries

Healthy boundaries are essential in marriage as they provide a framework for mutual respect and personal well-being. By understanding your own limits and what you need to feel secure and respected, you can clearly communicate these boundaries to your spouse. This clarity helps prevent misunderstandings and ensures that both partners are aware of each other's expectations and comfort zones. Setting healthy boundaries allows each person to maintain their individuality while nurturing the relationship, creating a balanced dynamic where both partners feel valued and understood. This mutual respect forms the foundation of a strong, resilient marriage.

Moreover, establishing and maintaining healthy boundaries prevents resentment from accumulating due to unmet needs or crossed lines. When boundaries are clearly defined and honored, it minimizes the likelihood of conflicts arising from feelings of neglect or disrespect. Both partners are more likely to feel satisfied and content, knowing that their personal needs and limits are recognized and upheld. This practice of respecting each other's boundaries fosters a positive and supportive atmosphere, encouraging open communication and deeper emotional connection. By prioritizing healthy boundaries, couples can navigate the complexities of marriage with greater ease and harmony, ultimately strengthening their bond.

Developing Conflict Resolution

Conflict resolution in your relationship is greatly enhanced by self-awareness, particularly regarding your triggers and stress responses. When you know what typically provokes a strong emotional reaction and how you usually respond under stress, you can approach disagreements with a calmer and more deliberate mindset. This self-awareness helps you recognize when you might be overreacting or misinterpreting your partner's actions, allowing you to pause and reflect before responding. By managing your emotional responses effectively, you can prevent unnecessary escalation of conflicts, keeping discussions productive rather than confrontational.

Moreover, understanding your own conflict resolution style enables you to adopt a more collaborative approach to resolving issues. Instead of defaulting to defensive or aggressive behaviors, you can focus on finding common ground and working together to address the root causes of disagreements. This approach fosters a spirit of teamwork and mutual respect, as both partners feel heard and valued. By prioritizing constructive dialogue and actively seeking solutions that satisfy both parties, couples can strengthen their relationship and build a more resilient partnership. Effective conflict resolution, grounded in selfawareness, transforms challenges into opportunities for growth and deeper connection.

Enhancing Empathy for Your Spouse

Greater empathy for your partner is fostered through a deep understanding of your own experiences and emotions. When you are aware of your feelings and the situations that shape them, you can better relate to your spouse's emotional landscape. This self-awareness allows you to recognize and validate their feelings, fostering a deeper connection. By empathizing with your partner, you show that you understand and care about their experiences, creating a nurturing environment where both partners feel heard and valued.

This enhanced empathy strengthens the emotional bond between spouses, promoting a more compassionate and supportive relationship. When you can genuinely share in your partner's joys and sorrows, it builds trust and intimacy, reinforcing the sense of partnership. Empathy encourages open communication, as both partners feel safe to express their true selves without fear of judgment. This mutual understanding and compassion lay the groundwork for a resilient marriage, where challenges are met with unity and shared strength. By cultivating greater empathy through self-awareness, couples can deepen their emotional connection and create a more loving and supportive marriage.

Standing in Knowledge of Your Purpose

Knowing your purpose involves seeking God's guidance through prayer, Scripture, and reflection. It means understanding the unique gifts and talents He has bestowed upon you and how you can use them to serve Him and others. When you and your spouse are aligned in your purposes, you create a powerful synergy that can achieve great things for God's kingdom. This alignment reduces conflicts that arise from differing goals and provides a unified vision for your future together. It encourages each partner to pursue their individual callings while also supporting and uplifting their spouse's mission.

A marriage grounded in shared purpose also offers resilience against life's inevitable trials. When challenges arise, couples with a clear understanding of their divine mission can draw strength from their commitment to God's plan. They can remind each other of their higher calling and find solace in the knowledge that their struggles are part of a larger, divine narrative. This perspective shifts the focus from immediate difficulties to long-term spiritual growth and fulfillment. It allows couples to navigate hardships with faith and perseverance, knowing that they are working together towards a God-ordained purpose.

Knowing Your Vocation

Knowing the vocation to which you are called is vital for leading a fulfilling and harmonious life. When individuals align themselves with their God-given vocation, whether as a teacher, mechanic, firefighter, or any other profession, they operate in a state of harmony with themselves. This alignment brings a sense of purpose and satisfaction that transcends mere financial gain. Making vocational decisions based solely on economic factors or the pursuit of money can lead to an unfulfilled and unhappy existence. This discontentment can seep into one's personal life, affecting relationships and home life. As the Apostle Paul admonishes us, it is essential to know the vocation with which we are called, as this understanding is foundational to living a life of purpose and joy.

In the context of marriage, being aligned with one's vocation can significantly impact the health and happiness of the relationship. When both partners are engaged in work that they find meaningful and fulfilling, they are more likely to bring positive energy and contentment into their home life. Conversely, if one or both partners are dissatisfied with their vocational choices, this can lead to stress, frustration, and even resentment, which can strain the relationship. While it is not necessary for both partners to share the same vocation, having a partner who is supportive and thinks positively about your vocation is crucial. This support can manifest in various ways, from providing emotional encouragement to showing interest and appreciation for the work you do.

Additionally, having a partner in a similar vocation can be a bonus, offering a unique level of support and understanding. Shared vocational experiences can foster a deeper connection and mutual respect, as both partners can relate to the challenges and rewards associated with their profession. However, even if the vocations are different, the key is mutual respect and support for each other's professional paths. When partners understand and appreciate the significance of each other's work, they create a supportive and nurturing environment that allows both individuals to thrive in their respective vocations. This mutual support not only enhances personal fulfillment but also strengthens the marital bond, contributing to a more harmonious and God-centered marriage.

Some women feel a primary calling to be wives and mothers, choosing to focus on nurturing their families rather than pursuing a professional career. This preference aligns with the expectations of some men who value and support traditional roles within the household. It's crucial for couples to have open and honest discussions about these expectations and roles before marriage to ensure mutual understanding and agreement. Establishing this clarity beforehand helps prevent potential conflicts and misunderstandings, laying a foundation for a harmonious and supportive partnership that honors each individual's values and aspirations.

Sharing Your Goals

Shared goals in marriage are vital for fostering unity and direction, and knowing yourself is key to identifying and aligning these goals with your spouse. When you have a clear understanding of your personal aspirations, values, and what you seek to achieve in life, you can communicate these effectively to your partner. This self-awareness enables both of you to discuss and harmonize your individual ambitions, creating a cohesive and shared vision for your future together. By aligning your goals, you ensure that you both are on the same path, working towards common objectives that reflect your mutual values and aspirations.

This alignment of goals not only strengthens your partnership but also enhances your ability to support and motivate each other. With a shared vision, both partners can contribute to and celebrate each other's successes, fostering a deeper sense of teamwork and mutual satisfaction. It helps in making joint decisions regarding important aspects of life, such as career choices, financial planning, and family matters, ensuring that both partners are invested in the same outcomes. By knowing yourself and understanding your spouse's goals, you create a strong foundation for a fulfilling and purpose-driven marriage, where both partners feel understood, valued, and united in their journey together.

Step 6: Seek Wise Counsel

Courtship is a pivotal period in any relationship, laying the groundwork for a potentially lifelong partnership. During this time, the importance of seeking wise counsel cannot be overstated. Whether from trusted family members, friends, or professionals, wise counsel can offer invaluable insights and guidance that help ensure the success and health of a relationship.

It is essential to exercise discernment in where you seek advice. While single individuals or those in unhappy relationships may offer well-intentioned advice, their perspectives could be colored by their own negative experiences. They may inadvertently project their own hurts, fears, or biases onto your situation, potentially leading to advice that may not align with your needs or goals. Therefore, while considering advice from various sources can be beneficial, it's crucial to prioritize counsel from individuals who demonstrate wisdom, objectivity, and a positive track record in their own relationships. This approach ensures that the guidance you receive is constructive and supportive of your journey towards a healthy and fulfilling partnership. Here are several compelling reasons why seeking wise counsel during courtship is crucial.

Objective Perspective

One of the most significant benefits of seeking wise counsel is the objective perspective they provide. When you are deeply involved in a relationship, emotions can cloud your judgment, making it difficult to see potential issues or strengths clearly. A wise counselor, detached from emotional entanglement, can offer a balanced and impartial viewpoint. They can help you identify dynamics that might be problematic or beneficial, which you might overlook. This objectivity is essential in making informed decisions about the future of the relationship.

However, it's important to remember that while wise counselors provide valuable insights, they may not fully understand the intricacies of your unique relationship dynamics or personal feelings. Trusting your own intuition and inner knowing is equally crucial. You are the ultimate authority in your own life and relationship. While considering counsel, it's essential to maintain a balance between external advice and internal guidance. Reflecting on how advice resonates with your values and instincts ensures that you make decisions that are authentic and true to yourself. Ultimately, integrating both external wisdom and internal discernment enables you to navigate courtship with clarity and confidence, ensuring that you and your partner build a relationship grounded in mutual understanding and respect.

Experience and Wisdom

Wise counselors bring a wealth of experience and knowledge about relationships, which can be incredibly beneficial during courtship. Their extensive life experiences enable them to offer practical and insightful advice on navigating the complexities of a relationship. They can share lessons learned from their own experiences or those of others, helping you avoid common pitfalls and embrace practices that foster a healthy relationship. This wisdom can be a guiding light, steering you through the often turbulent waters of courtship.

Guidance on Values and Compatibility

Assessing compatibility in terms of values, goals, and long-term aspirations is crucial for a lasting relationship. Wise counselors can help you and your partner evaluate whether your life goals and values are aligned. This guidance is vital for ensuring that you are building a relationship on a solid foundation. Compatibility in core areas such as faith, family, and future ambitions significantly impacts the long-term success of a relationship. Counselors can help you address these topics thoughtfully and comprehensively.

Conflict Resolution Skills

Effective conflict resolution skills are foundational to the success of any relationship, and seeking wise counsel can provide invaluable guidance in this area.

Counselors can teach you practical strategies for managing and resolving conflicts in a constructive manner. Learning to navigate disagreements with respect, empathy, and open communication is essential for preventing minor issues from escalating into significant problems. These skills not only foster a harmonious courtship but are crucial for maintaining a cooperative and supportive partnership throughout your entire relationship journey.

It is important to seek counsel from individuals who advocate for working through conflicts in relationships. In today's fast-paced world, there is often a tendency to discard relationships at the first sign of trouble. However, wise counselors emphasize that conflict is a natural part of any relationship and can be an opportunity for growth and deeper understanding between partners. They can help you recognize that disagreements do not automatically indicate a doomed relationship but rather a chance to strengthen your bond through mutual respect and compromise.

Each individual in a relationship comes with their own background, upbringing, and life experiences. Wise counsel acknowledges the complexity of these differences and encourages couples to allow time and effort to work through their differences. Rushing to judgment or succumbing to societal pressures like cancel culture can undermine the potential for a fulfilling and lasting relationship. By nurturing patience and commitment, couples can build resilience and trust, laying the groundwork for a relationship that thrives despite challenges and differences.

Emotional Support

Courtship is undeniably an emotionally intense phase, filled with excitement, uncertainty, and vulnerability. Having a trusted advisor during this time plays a crucial role in providing much-needed emotional support. A wise counselor can offer a safe space for you to express your feelings openly and honestly. They listen without judgment and help you process complex emotions, enabling you to make decisions with clarity and a balanced perspective. This emotional support is invaluable in alleviating stress and anxiety that often accompany the uncertainties of courtship, allowing you to navigate your relationship with greater confidence and understanding.

During frustrating or challenging times in courtship, it's natural to vent your frustrations to a counselor or advisor. However, it's essential to communicate clearly that you are venting and seeking emotional release rather than making definitive judgments about your partner or the relationship. Wise counselors recognize the difference between venting and making decisions, ensuring that their guidance remains objective and grounded in understanding rather than knee-jerk reactions to emotional outbursts. It's also important to maintain a balanced perspective in your discussions with advisors. While it's crucial to address concerns or frustrations, it's equally important to highlight and appreciate the positive qualities and aspects of your potential spouse. This balanced approach ensures that your counselor gets a complete picture of your relationship dynamics and can offer well-rounded advice that considers both challenges and strengths.

Ultimately, a wise counselor serves as a sounding board during uncertain times in courtship, offering comfort, reassurance, and practical insights. By fostering open communication and trust, they help you navigate the emotional highs and lows of courtship with resilience and clarity. Their guidance supports you in making informed decisions that align with your values and aspirations, fostering a relationship that is built on mutual understanding, respect, and emotional wellbeing.

Spiritual Guidance

Spiritual advisors play a pivotal role in offering insights and guidance that align with your faith, particularly in fostering a Christ-centered relationship during courtship. Their wisdom and counsel are instrumental in helping you navigate decisions that honor your spiritual values and beliefs. By providing guidance that aligns with Christ's teachings and principles, spiritual advisors ensure that your relationship develops in a manner that reflects your commitment to faith. This approach not only strengthens your individual spiritual journey but also deepens the spiritual connection between you and your partner, laying a solid foundation for a meaningful and Christ-centered relationship.

Embracing a Christ-centered perspective with the guidance of spiritual advisors ensures that your courtship journey reflects biblical principles of love, respect, and mutual understanding. They can offer practical advice on integrating prayer, scripture, and faith-based discussions into your relationship dynamics. This spiritual guidance encourages both partners to prioritize spiritual growth and unity, fostering a shared commitment to living out Christ's teachings in their relationship. By grounding your courtship in a Christcentered approach, you cultivate a relationship that is rooted in faith, grace, and God's guidance, enriching your journey towards a loving and fulfilling partnership.

The role of spiritual advisors extends beyond mere guidance; they provide a supportive environment where you and your partner can explore and deepen your faith together. By encouraging prayer, worship, and spiritual reflection, they nurture a spiritual bond that strengthens your relationship's resilience and depth. Spiritual advisors help you discern God's will for your relationship, guiding you towards decisions that honor Him and align with your shared faith values. This spiritual foundation not only enriches your courtship experience but also prepares you both for a future built on a steadfast commitment to Christ and His teachings.

Red Flags Identification

An experienced counselor brings a critical eye to your relationship, capable of identifying potential red flags that might go unnoticed amidst the excitement of courtship. These warning signs could manifest as concerning behaviors, conflicting attitudes, or recurring patterns that have the potential to escalate into significant issues over time. By recognizing these early indicators, you gain the opportunity to address them proactively, thereby safeguarding yourself from future heartache and nurturing a relationship that is healthy and sustainable in the long term.

It's important to remember that counselors provide guidance based on the information you share about your potential partner. While their insights are valuable, they may not possess a comprehensive understanding of your partner beyond what you disclose. This limited perspective can sometimes lead to partial judgments or recommendations that might not fully align with the nuanced reality of your relationship. Therefore, while considering their counsel objectively, it's crucial to maintain your own understanding and intuition about your partner. You are the one who knows them best, with firsthand knowledge of their character, values, and motivations.

To enrich the advice you receive, consider involving your advisors in getting to know your potential spouse personally. Encourage interactions where they can observe your partner's behavior, values, and interactions firsthand. This allows them to form a more informed and balanced perspective, providing you with more accurate guidance that considers both your insights and their observations. By fostering this collaborative approach between you, your potential partner, and your counselors, you can make more informed decisions about your relationship while ensuring that you remain grounded in your understanding of each other's true selves.

Personal Growth

Engaging with wise counsel plays a crucial role in fostering personal growth during courtship and beyond. Counselors provide a supportive environment where you can reflect on your behaviors, attitudes, and communication styles. Through this introspection, they encourage self-awareness and personal development, helping you identify and address blind spots that may impact your relationship. This process of self-discovery not only enhances your ability to navigate challenges within the relationship but also contributes to your overall well-being and maturity.

It's essential to seek counsel from individuals who challenge you and provide objective feedback, rather than merely agreeing with your perspective. Having advisors who are willing to offer constructive criticism and hold you accountable is invaluable. They can help you recognize patterns of behavior or thought that may be detrimental to your relationship, prompting growth and positive change. By embracing diverse viewpoints and feedback from trusted counselors, you cultivate a deeper understanding of yourself and your interactions with others. This holistic approach to personal growth ensures that you enter into and sustain a relationship with authenticity, humility, and a commitment to continuous improvement.

Encouragement and Accountability

Wise counselors offer invaluable support by providing encouragement and holding you accountable to your commitments and relationship goals. Their guidance helps you maintain focus and motivation, especially during challenging times in your courtship. Knowing that you have someone who genuinely wants to see you succeed in your relationship endeavors can be incredibly reassuring and empowering. They provide a steady source of encouragement, reinforcing your dedication to building a healthy and fulfilling partnership.

It's essential to surround yourself with individuals who prioritize your relationship's well-being and share in your desire for its success. Seeking counsel from exboyfriends or girlfriends, even if they are now close friends, can introduce complexities and biases that may not serve your current relationship goals. These individuals may have their own perspectives shaped by past experiences with you, which could inadvertently influence their advice. Instead, choosing counselors who are impartial and focused on your present relationship dynamics ensures that you receive objective guidance aligned with your current aspirations and challenges. This approach fosters a supportive environment where you can confidently pursue growth and resilience in your courtship, guided by wisdom and encouragement from those who have your relationship's best interests at heart.

Building a Strong Foundation

Ultimately, seeking wise counsel helps you build a strong and stable foundation for your relationship. By taking the necessary steps to understand and address important issues during courtship, you increase the likelihood of a successful and enduring marriage. Wise counsel ensures that you are well-prepared to enter into a lifelong partnership with confidence and clarity, setting the stage for a fulfilling and harmonious relationship.

The benefits of seeking wise counsel during courtship are manifold. From providing an objective perspective to fostering personal growth, wise counselors play a crucial role in guiding couples toward a successful and healthy relationship. By embracing the wisdom and guidance of trusted advisors, couples can navigate the complexities of courtship with greater ease and assurance, building a strong foundation for their future together.

Step 7: Prioritize Compatibility

Shared Faith

One of the most critical aspects of compatibility in courting is having a shared faith. This common spiritual foundation is essential for several reasons. Firstly, it ensures that both partners are aligned in their beliefs about God, salvation, and how they live out their faith daily. When both partners share the same faith, they can support each other's spiritual growth through prayer, Bible study, and participation in church activities. This mutual support helps to foster a deeper spiritual connection and a sense of unity that can carry the couple through life's challenges.

Additionally, a shared faith promotes unity in worship and prayer, creating a strong spiritual bond. This unity is particularly important when it comes to raising children. Parents who share the same faith can provide consistent spiritual guidance and model a life of faith for their children, ensuring that the family grows together in their relationship with God. This spiritual harmony sets a positive example and creates a stable and nurturing environment for children to develop their own faith.

The Bible provides clear guidance on the importance of spiritual alignment in relationships, particularly in marriage. In the Old Testament, God instructed the

Israelites not to marry foreign women who worshiped other gods, warning that such unions could lead them astray and cause them to follow false deities (Deuteronomy 7:3-4, Nehemiah 13:25-27). This principle is echoed in the New Testament where Paul advises believers not to be unequally yoked with unbelievers (2 Corinthians 6:14). The underlying message in both scriptures is the importance of maintaining spiritual integrity and devotion to God, ensuring that one's partner shares the same faith and commitment. This spiritual compatibility helps to build a strong, unified relationship that honors God and prevents the influence of conflicting beliefs and values.

Aligned Values and Beliefs

Having aligned values and beliefs is another cornerstone of a compatible relationship. When partners share similar moral and ethical standards, they are less likely to encounter conflicts over important decisions and lifestyle choices. This alignment strengthens the decision-making process, as both partners are guided by the same principles. Whether it's deciding on financial matters, career paths, or parenting styles, having shared values ensures that both partners are on the same page and can work together harmoniously.

Aligned values also foster a unified vision for family life and long-term goals. Couples who share similar beliefs about what is important in life are more likely to work together towards common objectives, such as building a strong family, contributing to their community, or growing in their faith. This unity helps to create a sense of purpose and direction in the relationship, which can be incredibly fulfilling and motivating for both partners.

It is wise to discuss areas like health care, education, and parenting. For example, if one parent strongly believes in the efficacy of western medicine while the other prefers herbal remedies, this disparity can lead to significant conflicts when making health-related decisions for the family. Similarly, differing views on schooling—such as one partner advocating for homeschooling while the other supports public schooling—can create tension and disagreement. It is essential to discuss these practical values during the courtship phase to understand each other's perspectives and find common ground. Such discussions help to identify potential areas of conflict early on and enable couples to navigate these differences proactively. Assuming that a partner's views will change after marriage is often unrealistic and can lead to disappointment and friction. Clear communication and mutual respect for each other's values are foundational for a strong and unified marriage.

Emotional Compatibility

Emotional compatibility is vital for a deep and meaningful relationship. It involves understanding and responding to each other's emotional needs and responses. When partners are emotionally compatible, they can effectively communicate and resolve conflicts in a healthy manner. This understanding promotes emotional intimacy and strengthens the bond between them. Emotional compatibility also enhances the couple's ability to support each other during challenging times, creating a resilient and loving partnership.

Moreover, emotional compatibility encourages a deeper understanding of each other's personalities and backgrounds. Knowing your partner's triggers, vulnerabilities, and past experiences allows for more empathetic and supportive interactions. This awareness fosters a safe and nurturing environment where both partners can express themselves freely and authentically. Over time, this emotional connection deepens, creating a strong foundation for a lasting relationship.

Intellectual Compatibility

Intellectual compatibility is another important factor in a thriving relationship. It involves the ability to engage in stimulating and meaningful conversations, sharing ideas, and respecting each other's viewpoints. Intellectual compatibility fosters mutual respect and admiration, which are essential for a healthy relationship. When partners can discuss and explore various topics together, they encourage each other's growth and learning, enriching their lives and their relationship.

Additionally, intellectual compatibility can enhance the couple's ability to collaborate on problem-solving and decision-making. Partners who think similarly or complement each other's thinking styles are better equipped to navigate life's challenges together. This shared intellectual connection also promotes a sense of companionship and camaraderie, making the relationship more fulfilling and enjoyable.

A good conversation serves as a constant companion throughout life, including into old age. Engaging in stimulating discussions ensures that both partners feel mentally challenged and respected, fostering a deep connection and mutual admiration. Without intellectual compatibility, one partner may feel unstimulated or undervalued, leading to boredom and potential dissatisfaction. Respect for each other's intellect and the ability to engage in meaningful dialogue helps maintain interest and enthusiasm in the relationship, contributing to its overall health and longevity. Thus, prioritizing intellectual compatibility during courtship can significantly enhance the quality and endurance of the partnership.

Lifestyle Preferences

Compatibility in lifestyle preferences is crucial for harmony in daily life. This includes preferences for activities, social interactions, and personal space. Ensuring that both partners have compatible lifestyles can prevent friction and misunderstandings. For instance, if one partner prefers a quiet, home-centered life while the other enjoys a busy social calendar, conflicts can arise. Finding a balance that respects both partners' preferences is essential for a happy and balanced life together.

The amount of personal space individuals prefer in relationships is one of the most underrated yet crucial aspects of compatibility. If one partner prefers a lot of alone time while the other craves constant togetherness, this mismatch can lead to significant dissatisfaction and conflict. It's important to understand that differing needs for personal space do not necessarily indicate a lack of love or commitment. Some individuals, particularly introverts, need alone time to recharge and maintain their well-being. Conversely, those who thrive on social interaction may feel neglected or unloved if their partner frequently seeks solitude.

Identifying these preferences during the courting process is essential to prevent future disappointments and misunderstandings. Open discussions about personal space can help both partners understand and respect each other's needs. This awareness allows for the creation of a balanced relationship dynamic where both individuals feel valued and fulfilled. Recognizing and accommodating these differences early on can lead to a more harmonious and satisfying partnership, reducing the potential for resentment and ensuring that both partners' emotional needs are met.

Lifestyle compatibility also involves aligning on longterm living arrangements, such as whether to live in a city or the countryside, and preferences for climate. These decisions impact daily life and overall happiness, so it is important to discuss and agree on these aspects during the courting process. By ensuring compatibility in lifestyle preferences, couples can create a harmonious and enjoyable life together, reducing potential sources of conflict.

Long-term Goals and Ambitions

Aligning on long-term goals and ambitions is vital for a cohesive and forward-looking relationship. When both partners share similar aspirations for their careers, family, and personal development, they can work together as a team to achieve these goals. This alignment promotes teamwork and cooperation, allowing the couple to support each other's ambitions and dreams. Having shared long-term goals also helps to keep the couple focused and united, navigating life's challenges with a clear sense of direction.

Moreover, having aligned goals reduces the risk of divergent paths causing strain on the relationship. When partners have different aspirations that are not compatible, it can lead to conflicts and feelings of resentment. By ensuring that both partners are aligned in their long-term goals, the relationship can flourish with a shared vision and purpose, creating a strong and united partnership.

Cultural Backgrounds

Cultural compatibility is an important aspect of a harmonious relationship. Understanding and appreciating each other's cultural heritage promotes unity and respect within the relationship. This includes traditions, celebrations, and family practices. Navigating cultural differences harmoniously can enrich the relationship, providing opportunities for learning and growth. It is important for partners to discuss and respect each other's cultural backgrounds, ensuring that these differences are acknowledged and valued.

Cultural compatibility also plays a role in how couples navigate their social lives and family dynamics. Understanding and appreciating each other's cultural perspectives can help prevent misunderstandings and conflicts. By fostering an environment of respect and inclusion, couples can build a strong foundation for a loving and supportive relationship.

If one partner wishes to celebrate Biblical holidays like Passover to honor Christ's sacrifice, recognizing the pagan aspects of modern holidays like Christmas and Easter, while the other partner loves and cherishes Christmas, this misalignment can lead to significant dissatisfaction. Celebrations are an integral part of marriage, serving as moments of bonding and shared joy. Differing views on which holidays to celebrate and how to observe them can create tension and conflict.

These differences reflect deeper values and beliefs that need to be reconciled for a harmonious relationship. Discussing and understanding each other's perspectives on holidays during the courting process is crucial to ensure mutual understanding and find a way to celebrate that honors both partners' convictions.

Financial Compatibility

Financial compatibility is essential for a stable and secure relationship. Ensuring agreement on spending habits, saving goals, and financial management can prevent conflicts and misunderstandings. Partners who share similar financial values are better equipped to make joint financial decisions and plan for their future together. This alignment promotes transparency and trust, reducing stress and potential conflicts related to money.

Moreover, financial compatibility supports a stable and secure financial future. When partners have a shared approach to managing finances, they can work together towards common financial goals, such as buying a home, saving for retirement, or supporting their children's education. This shared financial vision helps to create a sense of security and stability in the relationship, contributing to overall happiness and wellbeing.

Physical Compatibility

There is often a debate on whether someone can marry someone they are not physically attracted to. Initial attraction is important as it is often the first signal that this person may be a potential mate. This initial spark can create a desire to get to know the person better and can help foster an emotional connection. While physical attraction serves as an important indicator, it should not be the sole criterion for choosing a partner.

Relationships based solely on physical attraction often lack depth and may not stand the test of time when faced with life's challenges.

Physical attraction can and will grow as love grows. As we get to know people better, small things that may have initially bothered us might ultimately fade away. Understanding a person's character, values, and personality can enhance their attractiveness. Over time, the emotional and spiritual bond formed with a partner can significantly increase physical attraction. Conversely, someone we are overwhelmingly attracted to at the beginning might lose their allure if we discover we are not compatible on other levels or if we observe negative character traits in them.

Therefore, while it is important not to ignore physical compatibility, it should not be the foundation of a relationship. It can sometimes be the biggest illusion, leading us to overlook more critical aspects like character, values, and emotional compatibility. True and lasting love encompasses more than just physical attraction; it is built on mutual respect, shared values, and a deep emotional connection. Thus, a balanced approach, considering both physical attraction and other crucial factors, is essential in the courting process.

Evaluating Chemistry

In modern dating, people often justify having sex before marriage as a way to test sexual compatibility. However, this rationale often serves as an excuse to engage in premarital sex. Sexual compatibility is undoubtedly important in marriage, but it does not need to be "tried on" before exchanging vows. True chemistry is something that can be felt through emotional and physical connection, often evident simply by being in close proximity to someone. If you feel an intense draw to your partner, that is a sign of chemical attraction.

Being physically attracted to your mate also plays a significant role in sexual chemistry. This attraction can enhance the overall connection and anticipation in the relationship, fostering a deeper bond. However, physical attraction alone is not enough to sustain a marriage. The strength of love shared between partners is critical for sexual chemistry. When two people share a profound love and respect for each other, they naturally enjoy the intimacy of sexual union. This connection is not solely based on physical attributes but also on emotional and spiritual alignment.

Sexual preferences and boundaries can and should be discussed during the courting process. For example, if a partner has specific beliefs or boundaries regarding certain sexual acts, it is essential to communicate these openly and respectfully. Overall, the combination of chemical draw, physical attraction, and a strong foundation of love and mutual respect forms the recipe for a positive sexual experience in marriage. These elements together ensure that the intimacy shared is meaningful, fulfilling, and aligned with the couple's values and commitments.

Parenting Styles and Family Planning

Compatibility in parenting styles and family planning is crucial for raising children and creating a harmonious family life. Aligning expectations for raising children and family size ensures consistency in parenting methods and disciplinary approaches. This alignment promotes a cohesive and nurturing family environment, providing stability and support for children's development.

Additionally, having compatible parenting styles reduces potential conflicts and stress related to childrearing. When both partners share similar approaches to parenting, they can work together as a team to provide the best possible upbringing for their children. This shared vision for family life enhances the overall harmony and happiness of the relationship, creating a strong and loving family unit.

Conclusion

Prioritizing compatibility in courting is essential for building a strong foundation for a healthy, fulfilling, and God-centered marriage. Ensuring compatibility in areas such as faith, values, emotions, intellect, lifestyle, goals, culture, finances, physical needs, and parenting styles minimizes potential conflicts and promotes mutual respect. By focusing on compatibility, couples can create a harmonious and supportive partnership that enhances their overall happiness and well-being. This strong foundation allows the relationship to flourish and grow, reflecting God's design and intention for marriage.

Step 8: Set Healthy Boundaries

Boundaries in courting are crucial for maintaining the integrity of the relationship and ensuring it aligns with spiritual values. Courting should be a time of intentional, respectful interaction, where both partners seek to understand each other and build a foundation for a potential future together. This period should be characterized by a commitment to upholding moral and ethical standards that honor God. Clear boundaries help to create a safe space for both individuals, preventing premature intimacy and fostering a deeper emotional and spiritual connection.

I recently came across a post in a singles social media group that read as follows: "*I found my Rib. I came here a few months ago in joy and gladness to announce my search was over. Yet....we rushed. We slipped, and now.....she's not even talking to me anymore. Matter of fact, she's acting different altogether and basically just ended our courtship. When courting, it's best to keep it by the scriptures and get counsel because we all are carrying baggage that we don't want to ruin what Yah has given us. She was my second chance. Just use me as an example, fellas....KEEP IT SCRIPTURAL and BEDROOM UNDEFILED until marriage....*". This post highlights the importance of adhering to boundaries during courting. Rushing into physical intimacy can lead to emotional turmoil and the breakdown of the relationship, emphasizing the need to keep courting scriptural and seek guidance.

Loving someone is often not enough if we break boundaries. In courting, it is essential to follow guidelines that preserve the sanctity of the relationship and protect both partners from emotional harm. By keeping the relationship scriptural and seeking counsel, couples can navigate their baggage and avoid repeating past mistakes. Boundaries help ensure that both individuals remain focused on building a relationship based on mutual respect, spiritual alignment, and emotional safety. This disciplined approach to courting fosters a healthy environment where true love and commitment can flourish, paving the way for a strong and God-honoring marriage.

Establishing healthy boundaries in courting and relationships is essential for maintaining respect, emotional safety, and alignment with spiritual values. These boundaries help create a strong foundation for a relationship that honors God and promotes mutual growth and understanding. Here are several ways to establish these boundaries:

Define Relationship Goals and Intentions

The first step in setting healthy boundaries is to define the goals and intentions of the relationship. Discussing and agreeing on the purpose of your relationship is crucial. Is your relationship focused on spiritual growth, mutual respect, and long-term commitment? By clarifying these goals early on, both partners can ensure they are on the same page and are working towards a common vision. This foundation helps prevent misunderstandings and sets a clear direction for the relationship.

Practice Purity

Practicing purity within the courting process is crucial for maintaining a relationship that honors God and fosters true emotional and spiritual connection. While the strong feelings during courtship might make it seem certain that the person you are courting will be your future spouse, it's important to remember that nothing is set in stone until the vows are taken. Rationalizing premature sexual union based on the assumption of an inevitable marriage can lead to regret and a sense of defilement if the relationship doesn't progress as expected. Premature sexual intimacy can cause resentment and emotional turmoil, complicating the relationship's future potential.

During the courting process, patience and self-control are vital. The temptation to rush into physical intimacy can be strong, especially when the chemistry and attraction between partners are high. However, it is essential to keep the physical aspects of the relationship at a controlled level, avoiding intense sexual acts. Discussing and agreeing on boundaries for physical affection can help both partners maintain purity and focus on developing their emotional and spiritual bond. These conversations should emphasize mutual respect and the commitment to preserving each other's dignity and integrity until marriage.

By delaying sexual union until the wedding day, couples can ensure that their relationship is built on a solid foundation of trust, respect, and shared values. This approach helps to avoid the confusion and blurred lines that often accompany premature physical intimacy. When the courting process is rushed, the true essence of getting to know one another can be overshadowed by the physical aspects, potentially leading to misunderstandings and unfulfilled expectations. Keeping physical boundaries in check allows the couple to fully explore their compatibility, discuss future goals, and address any issues that may arise without the added complexity of a sexual relationship.

Ultimately, practicing purity in courtship helps couples to focus on building a deep and meaningful connection that goes beyond physical attraction. It fosters an environment where both partners can grow together spiritually and emotionally, ensuring that their commitment is based on more than just physical desire. By adhering to these principles, couples can enter into marriage with a clear conscience and a strong, untainted bond, ready to face the challenges of married life with a united and steadfast spirit.

Communication Boundaries

Establishing communication boundaries is crucial for fostering a healthy and honest relationship. Open and honest communication about needs, expectations, and concerns forms the backbone of a strong partnership. Practicing active listening and respecting each other's viewpoints, even when they differ, promotes mutual understanding, reduces conflicts, and strengthens the emotional bond between partners. By engaging in this type of communication, couples can navigate their relationship with greater clarity and empathy, ensuring that both partners feel heard and valued.

It's essential to be aware of each other's triggers and sensitivities. For instance, one partner might use curse words, which could be deeply offensive to the other. If this is the case, a candid discussion is necessary to address these issues. The person using such language will need to decide if they are willing to change to accommodate their partner's comfort. This conversation shouldn't be overlooked, as language and tone can significantly impact the emotional atmosphere of the relationship. Similarly, the tone of speech matters; some people may speak loudly and passionately, which might be overwhelming or sensitive for others. Recognizing and adjusting these aspects of communication can prevent misunderstandings and foster a more harmonious relationship.

Understanding communication styles is also critical. Some individuals tend to keep a lot of things to themselves, not fully communicating their thoughts or grievances. This can lead to significant problems down the road if not addressed early. For example, in a previous marriage, I experienced a situation where, despite minimal arguing, my partner was silently sweeping issues under the rug for years. This ultimately led to a painful realization in year nine of our ten-year marriage when she unleashed all of her pent up grievances. If you are someone who tends to keep things bottled up, it's important to recognize that doing so is not beneficial for the relationship. Transparency and openness are vital for long-term success and happiness in any partnership.

For those who have a partner with a tendency to withhold their thoughts and feelings, it is crucial to be intentional about encouraging them to open up. Regularly check in with each other, even if it seems like everything is fine because there is no arguing. Lack of visible conflict does not always equate to a healthy relationship. Ensuring that both partners feel comfortable expressing themselves openly can prevent the buildup of unresolved issues and contribute to a more satisfying and enduring relationship. By setting and maintaining healthy communication boundaries, couples can create a supportive environment where both individuals can thrive and grow together.

Fostering open and honest communication about needs, expectations, and concerns is vital for a healthy relationship. Practice active listening and respect each other's viewpoints, even when they differ. This approach promotes understanding, reduces conflicts, and strengthens the emotional bond between partners.

Emotional Boundaries

Establishing emotional boundaries is vital for cultivating a healthy and enduring relationship. Building emotional intimacy should be a gradual process, allowing both partners to share personal details and feelings at a comfortable pace. This measured approach ensures that emotional connections develop naturally and authentically, fostering a deeper understanding and trust between partners. Rushing this process can lead to superficial connections and misunderstandings, as each person may not fully comprehend the depth of the other's experiences and emotions.

Avoiding over-dependence on each other for emotional support too early in the relationship is equally important. While it is natural to seek comfort and solace from a partner, relying excessively on them can lead to emotional imbalance and strain the relationship. It is essential for each individual to maintain their emotional stability and sense of self, ensuring that they are not losing their identity within the partnership. This independence supports a more balanced relationship, where both partners can provide support without feeling overwhelmed or burdened by the other's emotional needs.

Maintaining a sense of individuality within a relationship contributes significantly to its overall health and longevity. By respecting each other's emotional boundaries, partners can ensure that they are growing together while still nurturing their personal development and well-being. This balance allows for a partnership where both individuals can thrive independently and as a unit, creating a harmonious and resilient relationship. Emotional boundaries, when respected and maintained, lay the foundation for a loving, supportive, and sustainable partnership, where both partners feel valued and understood.

Spiritual Boundaries

Establishing spiritual boundaries in a relationship involves setting a routine of praying together and studying scripture to deepen your spiritual bond. This practice fosters a mutual commitment to spiritual growth, helping partners align their relationship with God's will. By sharing these moments of spiritual intimacy, couples can cultivate a deeper connection that transcends the physical and emotional aspects of their relationship, creating a foundation rooted in shared faith and values.

Understanding your partner's spiritual beliefs is crucial in maintaining these boundaries. It is essential not to expect your partner to change their beliefs to match yours. While there may be areas where your partner is willing to change or compromise, these adjustments should be discussed openly and honestly. Ensure that any changes do not compromise your partner's core beliefs and that they feel comfortable and genuine about making them. Spirituality is a deeply personal and sensitive area, and clear boundaries must be established to respect each other's faith journey.

Certain spiritual beliefs can be deal breakers, and it is important to recognize and address these early in the relationship. For example, if a fundamental belief, such as the gospel and the resurrection of Jesus Christ, is a core part of your faith, it should be clearly communicated and understood as a non-negotiable aspect of your spirituality. Compromising on such foundational beliefs can lead to significant conflicts and dissatisfaction in the relationship. It is vital to remember that, despite the connection you might feel with a person, your spiritual integrity should not be compromised. Don't assume that you will change your partner's mind about important topics of faith.

In the pursuit of a spiritually aligned relationship, it is important to remember that there are many individuals who share similar beliefs and values. The saying "there are plenty of fish in the sea" applies here; it is possible to find someone who is equally yoked with your spiritual beliefs. By prioritizing spiritual compatibility and setting clear boundaries, you can ensure that your relationship is built on a solid foundation of mutual faith and respect, leading to a more fulfilling and harmonious partnership. Keep in mind, the goal of courtship is to find out if this is the right person for you, Not to fight to stay together. Once you do find out that this is the right person, then the goal is engagement, marriage, and to stay together 'until death does you part'.

Cleave Don't Cling

"Cleave, don't cling" encapsulates the biblical principle of forming a strong, unbreakable bond while maintaining individuality and healthy boundaries within a relationship. Unlike clinging, which denotes a needy and overly dependent attachment, cleaving signifies a deep, committed bond that respects each partner's autonomy and personal space. In a cleaved relationship, both individuals nurture their unity while also valuing their individuality and personal growth. This balance allows for mutual support and companionship without stifling each other's independence.

Excessive jealousy and the need for constant proximity are often signs of insecurity rather than genuine love. During the courting process, it's crucial to observe how each partner navigates their need for space and their reactions to the other's activities and friendships. Understanding these dynamics helps distinguish between healthy attachment and unhealthy clinginess.

Genuine love respects boundaries and encourages personal growth, whereas clinging can inhibit individual development and strain the relationship.

Recognizing the difference between clinging and cleaving is essential for both partners' emotional and relational health. It requires self-awareness and a commitment to nurturing a relationship based on mutual respect and trust. By fostering a cleaved bond, couples can navigate challenges with greater resilience and maturity, ensuring their relationship grows in strength and unity over time.

Time Boundaries

Time boundaries in a relationship are essential for maintaining individual growth, personal responsibilities, and the overall health of the partnership. Balancing time spent together and apart enables each partner to pursue their interests, friendships, and professional endeavors while fostering a strong connection with their significant other. It ensures that the relationship thrives on quality time rather than quantity alone, promoting a deeper understanding and appreciation of each other's needs.

Understanding a person's time patterns and values regarding time management is crucial for setting effective time boundaries. Factors like punctuality, prioritization of commitments, and scheduling preferences can significantly impact how partners navigate their shared time. Communicating openly about expectations regarding the amount of time spent together and apart helps prevent misunderstandings and allows both individuals to align their schedules in a way that respects each other's priorities and boundaries.

Effective time boundaries also involve recognizing and respecting each other's need for personal space and independence. It's about finding a balance that accommodates both partners' lifestyles and allows for individual fulfillment alongside a committed relationship. By establishing clear communication and mutual understanding around time boundaries, couples can cultivate a relationship that thrives on shared moments of connection and supports each other's personal growth and well-being.

Social Boundaries

Social boundaries play a crucial role in maintaining harmony and trust within a relationship. Agreeing on how to manage social situations, interactions with friends and family, and boundaries with people of the opposite gender ensures that both partners feel secure and respected. It's important to discuss and establish guidelines early on regarding friendships with expartners, as this can be a sensitive issue that affects the current relationship dynamics. While one partner may feel comfortable maintaining casual contact with exes, the other may prefer stricter boundaries or complete cessation of communication to prioritize the current relationship's emotional security.

Additionally, friendships with individuals of the opposite gender should be approached with transparency and mutual understanding. Different couples may have varying comfort levels regarding the extent and nature of these friendships. Open communication and mutual agreements about boundaries can prevent misunderstandings and build trust between partners. It's essential for each person to respect their partner's feelings and preferences regarding social interactions to foster a supportive and respectful relationship environment.

Maintaining friendships and activities outside the romantic relationship is equally important for individual growth and fulfillment. Encouraging each other to nurture friendships and pursue personal interests helps maintain a healthy balance between social connections and the intimate partnership. Setting clear boundaries around social events and engagements ensures that both partners have the freedom to participate in activities that bring them joy and fulfillment while supporting each other's need for independence and personal space. By respecting each other's social boundaries, couples can strengthen their bond and create a supportive foundation for a lasting and fulfilling relationship.

In addition to navigating social boundaries, discussing the amount of time spent with each other's families and the expectations around prioritizing the marital relationship over other family ties is crucial. Understanding each other's family dynamics, traditions, and the level of involvement expected can prevent conflicts and misunderstandings in the future. It's important to address how holidays, celebrations, and important family events will be handled once married, ensuring that both partners feel valued and respected in their roles as spouses.

Furthermore, discussing the balance between maintaining healthy family connections and prioritizing the marital relationship early on can set a foundation for mutual understanding and support. While it's natural to have strong family bonds, the marriage relationship should take precedence in decision-making and emotional support. If one partner struggles to prioritize the marital bond over relationships with parents or extended family members, it may indicate a need for ongoing communication and boundary-setting to ensure a healthy balance.

Addressing these topics during the courting process allows both partners to align their expectations and develop strategies for navigating potential challenges in family dynamics. It also fosters transparency and trust, laying the groundwork for a resilient and harmonious marital relationship where both partners feel valued, supported, and secure in their commitment to each other.

Boundaries in Conflict Resolution

Establishing and respecting boundaries is essential for fostering a healthy and harmonious relationship, especially when it comes to handling disagreements. Instead of striving to win arguments, prioritize respectful dialogue and mutual understanding. This approach allows both partners to express their feelings and perspectives without diminishing each other's emotions. Taking breaks during heated discussions can be beneficial, providing space to cool down and gather thoughts before continuing the conversation. This practice helps prevent conflicts from escalating and promotes constructive conflict resolution.

Recognizing and respecting each other's need for space during disagreements is crucial. People have different styles of managing conflict—some may prefer immediate discussion, while others require time to process independently. Respecting these boundaries ensures that both partners feel heard and valued, fostering an environment where conflict can be addressed with empathy and understanding. Open communication about preferred conflict resolution approaches promotes mutual respect and strengthens emotional connections.

Certain boundaries must never be crossed during conflicts. Physical aggression or verbal abuse is never acceptable and undermines trust and emotional safety in the relationship. Upholding clear boundaries against harmful behaviors is essential for maintaining respect and promoting a healthy conflict resolution process. By prioritizing respectful communication, understanding individual needs for space, and enforcing nonnegotiable boundaries during disagreements, couples can cultivate a relationship grounded in trust, empathy, and effective problem-solving.

Boundaries with Finances

Financial boundaries play a crucial role in laying a solid foundation for a healthy relationship. Openly discussing financial values, habits, and priorities early in the courting process helps partners understand each other's approach to money. This discussion should encompass topics such as spending habits, saving goals, debt management, and attitudes towards financial planning. By addressing these aspects upfront, couples can assess their compatibility and identify potential areas of concern before entering into a committed relationship.

Maintaining separate finances during the courting phase is often advisable to avoid premature financial entanglements. This approach allows each partner to retain financial independence and make individual decisions regarding their money without the pressure of shared responsibilities. It also fosters a sense of personal responsibility and accountability, which are essential traits for successful financial management as a couple in the future. While discussing financial boundaries, it's important to establish mutual understanding and agreement on how financial decisions will be made once the relationship progresses towards marriage.

Setting financial boundaries early on not only prevents conflicts but also promotes transparency and trust between partners. It encourages open communication about financial expectations, goals, and potential challenges that may arise in the future. By navigating financial discussions with honesty and respect, couples can create a framework for managing money together effectively, ensuring financial stability and harmony in their relationship.

Step 9: Utilize Truthful Communication

Open and honest communication during courtship is not merely a recommended practice but a cornerstone of building a relationship rooted in authenticity and mutual respect. Unlike casual dating, the purpose of courtship is to discern whether two individuals are compatible for a lifelong commitment such as marriage. This process hinges on both parties being their genuine selves and learning about each other's truest selves without pretense or facade. In casual dating, people often put on masks, trying to impress the other person. The men might do this to have sexual encounters, while the women might do this to have a man who will buy them things. Even if they have marriage in mind, they often go about it the wrong way, trying to impress rather than earnestly seeking the truth of each other to find out if it is a good fit from God.

Building trust through authenticity is crucial. When individuals share their thoughts, feelings, and experiences honestly, it demonstrates transparency and sincerity. Trust forms the foundation of a healthy relationship, and consistent communication helps strengthen this foundation from the early stages of courtship. Being open and truthful about flaws and insecurities, even those that might seem minor or insignificant, allows both partners to see each other as they truly are. This level of honesty might be daunting, as it requires vulnerability and the risk of rejection. However, it is this very vulnerability that can foster deep trust and a genuine connection. By presenting themselves authentically, both individuals can better assess if they are truly compatible for a lifelong partnership.

Honesty in communication helps in identifying potential deal-breakers early on. For instance, differing values, goals, or beliefs that might be overlooked or masked in casual dating can be brought to the forefront during courtship. This not only saves time but also prevents heartache in the long run. When individuals are open about their intentions, expectations, and limitations, it sets a clear and realistic foundation for the relationship. It is better to address and navigate these differences early on rather than discovering them after a commitment has been made. This approach ensures that the relationship is built on solid ground, with both partners fully aware of what they are committing to.

Understanding and Embracing True Selves

Understanding and embracing each other's true selves is a vital aspect of open and honest communication in courtship. Effective communication allows partners to gain deeper insights into each other's personalities, values, and beliefs. By sharing openly, individuals can learn about their partner's goals, aspirations, fears, and past experiences. This understanding helps both parties assess compatibility and alignment in various aspects of life, such as career goals, family values, and lifestyle preferences.

In casual dating, people often present an idealized version of themselves, aiming to impress and win over the other person. This can lead to misunderstandings and unmet expectations once the relationship progresses and the true selves of both individuals are revealed. In contrast, courtship encourages partners to be genuine and transparent from the beginning. This means discussing not only strengths and successes but also weaknesses and challenges. Such openness helps partners understand each other's realities and provides a solid basis for empathy and support.

Furthermore, embracing each other's true selves involves accepting and loving each other despite imperfections. This doesn't mean ignoring red flags or compromising on essential values, but rather recognizing that everyone has flaws and that a healthy relationship is built on mutual support and growth. By being honest about their past, present, and future aspirations, partners can create a safe space where they feel accepted and valued. This level of understanding and acceptance is crucial for building a strong emotional bond and ensuring long-term compatibility.

Building Trust Through Openness

Trust is foundational in any relationship, and open communication is its bedrock. When partners share their thoughts, emotions, and experiences honestly, it demonstrates transparency and sincerity. This openness fosters a sense of reliability and security, showing that each partner is willing to be vulnerable and truthful. By consistently communicating openly, partners signal that they have nothing to hide, which helps to dispel doubts and build a solid foundation of trust. The process of revealing one's true self—warts and all—reinforces the idea that the relationship is built on genuine connection rather than superficial impressions.

Trust grows as individuals reveal their vulnerabilities and truths. When one partner shares personal stories, fears, or insecurities, it invites the other to reciprocate with empathy and understanding. This mutual exchange of honest communication creates a deeper emotional bond. Partners begin to see each other as safe havens where they can be their authentic selves without fear of judgment. This level of emotional intimacy is crucial for developing a secure and stable connection. As trust deepens, partners are more likely to rely on each other for support and encouragement, further solidifying their bond.

Moreover, trust built on open communication helps navigate challenges and conflicts within the relationship. When both partners are confident that they can express their true feelings without repercussions, it enables them to address issues head-on.
Misunderstandings and disagreements can be resolved more effectively because there is a baseline of trust that the other person is being honest and has their best interests at heart. This approach not only resolves

conflicts but also strengthens the relationship, as each resolved conflict adds to the trust reservoir. Ultimately, open and honest communication is the key to building a relationship where trust flourishes, creating a secure and stable connection that can withstand the test of time.

The Need for Constructive Conflict Resolution

Resolving conflicts constructively is another significant benefit of open and honest communication during courtship. Honest communication enables couples to address conflicts and disagreements constructively. When issues arise, openly discussing concerns and feelings allows partners to find solutions together rather than allowing misunderstandings to escalate. It promotes active listening, empathy, and compromise, which are essential skills for navigating challenges in any relationship.

During the courtship phase, it is crucial to develop healthy ways to handle disagreements. This includes focusing on respectful dialogue and seeking resolution rather than victory. Agreeing on taking breaks during heated arguments to cool down and approach the issue calmly helps prevent escalation and promotes constructive problem-solving. Knowing when your partner needs space, and when to approach them to communicate issues, is important. Different people have different styles of handling conflict. Knowing the boundaries of when your partner needs space, and making sure your partner can respect your space in conflict, are essential for maintaining harmony.

Conflict resolution should focus on showing empathy towards the other person's thoughts and feelings, often even more than getting your own point across. When partners approach disagreements with empathy, they prioritize understanding and validating each other's perspectives over simply winning an argument. This empathetic approach fosters a sense of mutual respect and demonstrates that each partner values the other's emotions and viewpoints. By actively listening and acknowledging the other person's feelings, partners can create a supportive environment where both feel heard and respected, which is crucial for resolving conflicts constructively.

Recognizing that you are on the same team with the same goal is essential in any relationship. When conflicts arise, it's important to remember that both partners care for each other and want what is best for one another. Adopting a mindset of collaboration rather than competition helps in viewing conflicts as opportunities to grow together rather than battles to be won. If this foundation of mutual care and a shared goal is not present, the relationship lacks a solid basis for resolving disputes. Effective conflict resolution relies on the understanding that both partners are allies working towards a common objective: a healthy, loving, and supportive relationship.

In any relationship, conflicts are inevitable, and our loved ones can and will hurt us unintentionally at times. The ability to forgive is crucial for maintaining a strong and lasting bond. Forgiveness allows us to move past hurtful incidents and focus on the positive aspects of the relationship. Without forgiveness, resentment and bitterness can build up, creating emotional barriers that hinder open communication and trust. By forgiving, we acknowledge that everyone makes mistakes and that our commitment to the relationship is stronger than any individual transgression.

If we cannot forgive, the relationship will deteriorate like rust. Just as rust gradually weakens and destroys metal, holding onto grudges and unresolved conflicts can erode the foundation of a relationship. Over time, the accumulation of unresolved hurts can lead to emotional distance, diminished intimacy, and a lack of trust. Forgiveness is the antidote to this corrosive process; it enables healing and allows the relationship to grow and thrive despite challenges. Embracing forgiveness not only strengthens the bond between partners but also fosters a healthier, more resilient relationship capable of withstanding the inevitable ups and downs of life.

Understanding Each Other

Effective communication is the cornerstone of understanding in a relationship, enabling partners to delve deep into each other's personalities, values, and beliefs. By sharing openly, individuals reveal their true selves, including their aspirations, fears, and past experiences. This level of transparency fosters a genuine connection, allowing both partners to see and appreciate each other beyond surface-level interactions. It lays the groundwork for a relationship built on mutual respect and genuine knowledge of one another, essential for navigating the complexities of life together.

Understanding each other through open communication is crucial for assessing compatibility in key areas such as life goals, family values, and lifestyle choices. When partners discuss their dreams and ambitions, they can determine if their paths align and support each other's growth. Similarly, conversations about family values reveal how each person views relationships, parenting, and traditions, helping to identify potential areas of conflict or agreement. Lifestyle choices, including habits, interests, and daily routines, are also important to discuss, as they can significantly impact the harmony of the relationship.

Moreover, this understanding helps in identifying and addressing potential issues before they become significant problems. For example, if one partner's career aspirations require frequent relocations, while the other values stability and close family ties, discussing these differences early on can lead to finding a compromise or reevaluating the relationship's feasibility. By thoroughly understanding each other's core values and beliefs, partners can make informed decisions about their future together, ensuring that their relationship is grounded in a solid foundation of compatibility and mutual support.

Setting Expectations

Clear communication plays a pivotal role in defining expectations for the relationship, especially during the courtship phase. By discussing important topics such as the pace of the courtship, boundaries, future aspirations, and commitment levels, both partners can ensure they are aligned in their intentions. This clarity minimizes misunderstandings and helps build a solid foundation based on mutual understanding. When partners openly share their visions for the relationship, it becomes easier to navigate the journey together, making informed decisions that support their collective goals.

It is essential to discuss the pace of the courtship early on. Some individuals may prefer a slow, deliberate approach to get to know each other deeply before making significant commitments, while others might feel ready to move quickly towards engagement and marriage. Understanding and respecting each other's comfort levels with the pace of the relationship helps prevent feelings of being rushed or held back, fostering a more harmonious connection.

Equally important is setting expectations for roles within marriage. For instance, discussing whether the husband is expected to participate in household chores like cleaning and doing dishes, or if the wife is expected to contribute financially to the household, is crucial. These conversations help establish a baseline of mutual expectations, ensuring that both partners feel comfortable and valued in their roles. Addressing these practical aspects of daily life before marriage can help minimize future problems and foster a more equitable partnership.

Additionally, setting expectations for future aspirations and commitment levels is vital. Topics such as career goals, desire for children, financial planning, and lifestyle preferences should be openly discussed to ensure compatibility. By aligning on these crucial aspects, couples can build a relationship grounded in shared values and mutual support. This proactive approach to communication not only strengthens the bond between partners but also prepares them for a future together that is built on trust, respect, and a clear understanding of each other's needs and expectations.

Strengthening Emotional Intimacy

Openly sharing vulnerabilities, dreams, and desires deepens emotional intimacy between partners, creating a foundation of trust and mutual respect. This level of transparency fosters closeness and nurtures a supportive and fulfilling relationship. By being open about their innermost thoughts and feelings, couples can develop a deeper understanding of each other, strengthening their emotional bond. This sense of security and belonging is essential for maintaining a healthy and enduring partnership.

Emotional intimacy is particularly valued by women, who often prioritize emotional connection in their relationships. When they don't feel emotionally connected, they may become distant and cold, impacting the overall dynamics of the relationship. Conversely, men might feel unfulfilled physically when the emotional connection with their partner is lacking. Men often don't realize that the physical lack stems from an emotional disconnect, leading to misunderstandings and further distancing. Recognizing and addressing these underlying emotional needs is essential for restoring intimacy and harmony in the relationship. Recognizing this interplay between emotional and physical fulfillment is crucial for maintaining a balanced and satisfying relationship.

There are numerous ways to deepen emotional connection, such as engaging in meaningful conversations, spending quality time together, and showing appreciation for each other. Active listening and empathetic responses can significantly enhance emotional intimacy, making partners feel heard and understood. Additionally, sharing experiences, both joyful and challenging, can bring couples closer together, fostering a resilient and supportive bond. By prioritizing emotional intimacy, couples can create a nurturing environment where both partners feel valued, loved, and connected.

Improving Decision Making

Open communication enables informed decisionmaking as a couple. When partners openly share their thoughts and feelings, they create a platform for mutual understanding and respect. Whether it involves major life choices, such as career moves or financial investments, or everyday decisions, like household chores or weekend plans, honest conversations ensure that both partners' viewpoints are considered. This level of transparency fosters a sense of equality and collaboration, which is essential for a harmonious relationship.

By engaging in honest dialogue, couples can weigh the pros and cons of various options and make decisions that reflect their combined wisdom and shared values. This collaborative approach not only promotes unity and teamwork but also enhances each partner's sense of agency and contribution to the relationship. When decisions are made together, both partners are more likely to feel invested in the outcome, leading to greater satisfaction and stability.

Moreover, effective communication helps partners anticipate and navigate challenges together. When couples regularly discuss their goals, concerns, and aspirations, they can proactively address potential conflicts and plan for the future. This joint problemsolving approach equips partners to handle unexpected situations with resilience and adaptability. In essence, open communication strengthens the couple's bond, making them a formidable team capable of seizing opportunities and overcoming obstacles together.

Words and Actions

Many people emphasize that actions speak louder than words, and this belief holds considerable truth. Words are easy to say and can often be insincere, but actions reveal a person's true intentions and feelings. For instance, someone might constantly profess their love, yet their behavior—such as being disrespectful, avoiding spending time together, or showing a lack of commitment—can contradict their words. In these instances, their actions are a more accurate reflection of their true sentiments, revealing a disparity between what they say and what they truly mean.

However, there are situations where it is crucial to pay attention to words over actions. A person might be physically present, engage in intimacy, or be financially intertwined with you, yet verbally express that they do not want a committed relationship or marriage. In such cases, despite their actions suggesting a level of involvement, their words clearly indicate their lack of desire for a deeper commitment. It is essential to take their verbal declarations seriously, as they often communicate their genuine intentions more directly than their actions.

Ultimately, it is important to consider both words and actions in relationships. Words can provide clarity and express explicit intentions, while actions can demonstrate true feelings and commitment. By carefully observing and balancing both, one can gain a comprehensive understanding of another person's true intentions and feelings. This dual awareness helps in making informed decisions about the future of the relationship, ensuring that both partners' words and actions are in harmony.

Communicating God's Purpose

In relationships, it's essential to recognize that they are not just about serving our own needs but, more importantly, about serving God. This perspective shifts the focus from personal gratification to a higher calling, where both partners seek to fulfill God's purpose in their lives. Discussing how a relationship and potential marriage can aid in this spiritual journey is crucial. It allows both individuals to align their goals and actions with divine intentions, ensuring that their union is a blessing not only to each other but also to their broader community and God's kingdom.

Talking about your purpose in God's kingdom is vital in determining if the relationship is the right fit. Each person has a unique calling, and it's essential to understand how your partner's vision and mission complement your own. This conversation should delve into how you both envision your future in terms of ministry, community service, and personal spiritual growth. If your partner's personality and goals align with God's purpose for you, it strengthens the foundation of your relationship, making it more resilient and purpose-driven.

However, if you find that your partner's personality or life goals deter you from your God-given purpose, it may not be a good fit. This doesn't necessarily reflect poorly on either individual but highlights the importance of compatibility in spiritual and life missions. For instance, if one partner feels called to a life of missionary work while the other prefers a more settled life, these differences must be reconciled early on. Ignoring these fundamental disparities can lead to significant conflicts and spiritual dissatisfaction in the long run.

Thus, it is imperative to have open and honest discussions about how the relationship can serve God's purpose. This dialogue helps to set clear expectations and ensures that both partners are on the same page regarding their spiritual journey. It also helps to identify potential challenges and opportunities for growth, making it easier to support each other in fulfilling God's will. Ultimately, a relationship rooted in a shared commitment to God's purpose is likely to be more harmonious, fulfilling, and enduring.

Step 10: Trust God's Timing

In the journey of courtship and preparing for marriage, patience and trust in God's timing are invaluable virtues. While the initial excitement of meeting someone special may make it tempting to rush into decisions, it's essential to remember that our understanding may not align with God's perfect plan. Waiting on God's timing allows for a deeper discernment of whether this person is indeed the spouse you've been praying for. It involves trusting that God knows what is best for your life and relationship, even when circumstances may seem uncertain or challenging.

Trusting God's Sovereignty

Proverbs 3:5-6 admonishes, "Trust in the Lord with all thine heart; and lean not unto thine own understanding. In all thy ways acknowledge him, and he shall direct thy paths." This verse underscores the importance of placing our trust in God's wisdom and timing rather than relying solely on our own insights or desires. Waiting patiently allows us to align our will with God's perfect plan, knowing that His timing is always purposeful and best.

Trusting God's sovereignty in the context of courtship involves surrendering our desires and plans to His divine wisdom and timing. Proverbs 3:5-6 provides clear guidance on this principle, urging believers to place their trust wholeheartedly in the Lord rather than leaning solely on their own understanding. This scripture emphasizes that acknowledging God in all aspects of our lives—including courtship and relationships—ensures that He will direct our paths according to His perfect will. This foundational trust requires patience and humility, recognizing that God's timing is purposeful and aligned with His greater plans for our lives.

In practical terms, trusting God's sovereignty means seeking His guidance through prayer and discernment at every stage of courtship. It involves entrusting Him with our desires and expectations, knowing that He sees the bigger picture and understands what is best for us. This trust allows couples to navigate uncertainties and challenges with confidence, believing that God is actively involved in shaping their relationship for His glory and their mutual good. By aligning their hearts and decisions with God's Word and His leading, couples cultivate a relationship that honors Him and stands on a foundation of faith.

Moreover, trusting God's sovereignty in courtship fosters a mindset of dependence on Him rather than relying on human wisdom or external pressures. It encourages couples to prioritize spiritual growth and seek unity in purpose, recognizing that God's plans exceed their own understanding. This trust enables individuals to surrender control, resist rushing into decisions based on emotions or societal expectations, and patiently wait for God's timing to unfold His perfect plan. As Proverbs 3:5-6 teaches, trusting in the Lord with all our hearts involves a continual acknowledgment of His sovereignty and a steadfast commitment to follow His direction in all areas of life, including relationships.

Patience and Perseverance

Psalm 27:14 encourages us to "Wait on the Lord: be of good courage, and he shall strengthen thine heart: wait, I say, on the Lord." This powerful verse reminds us that patience is not a passive act but an active stance of trust and perseverance. In the context of courtship, waiting on the Lord involves more than just biding time; it requires cultivating courage and faith while believing in God's perfect timing. It means trusting that God is orchestrating each step of the journey towards a fulfilling and lasting relationship, even when the path seems uncertain or prolonged.

Embracing this active patience in courtship involves continuous personal and spiritual growth. As individuals, it's essential to seek God wholeheartedly, developing a deeper relationship with Him while preparing for the future He has planned. For couples, it means building a strong foundation of mutual faith and values, nurturing their connection through prayer, Bible study, and shared spiritual practices. This process of waiting on the Lord strengthens the heart, instilling resilience and confidence that God's plan is unfolding perfectly, even if it requires patience and perseverance.

Furthermore, Psalm 27:14's call to wait on the Lord with courage speaks to the importance of maintaining hope and steadfastness. In courtship, there can be moments of doubt, impatience, or external pressures that challenge the couple's commitment to God's timing. By relying on God's strength and trusting in His sovereignty, couples can navigate these challenges with unwavering faith. This trust not only fortifies the relationship but also ensures that the partnership is built on a foundation of divine guidance and purpose. Waiting on the Lord, therefore, becomes a powerful act of faith that paves the way for a God-centered, enduring marriage.

Seeking God's Guidance

Proverbs 16:9 reminds us, "A man's heart deviseth his way: but the Lord directeth his steps." This verse highlights the delicate balance between our human desire to plan and God's ultimate sovereignty over our lives. In the context of courtship, seeking God's guidance through prayer and discernment is crucial to ensure that each step taken aligns with His will. By acknowledging that God's ways are higher and His timing is perfect, couples can surrender their plans and trust in His divine direction. This surrender is a powerful act of faith, reinforcing that God's guidance is essential in every decision they make.

As couples navigate the complexities and joys of courtship, relying on God's guidance provides a sense of clarity and purpose. Prayer becomes a central practice, inviting God's wisdom into their relationship and decisions. By prioritizing prayer and seeking God's direction, couples build a foundation based on faith and mutual respect. This spiritual discipline fosters a deeper connection with God and each other, ensuring that their relationship is not merely driven by personal desires but is rooted in a shared commitment to follow God's will.

Moreover, trusting in God's timing and guidance cultivates patience and perseverance. In a world that often emphasizes instant gratification and quick results, waiting on the Lord requires a steadfast faith that His plan is unfolding perfectly. As couples seek God's guidance, they learn to navigate uncertainties with grace, knowing that God's direction is leading them towards a fulfilling and purposeful relationship. This reliance on God not only strengthens their bond but also prepares them for a marriage that is centered on divine guidance, shared values, and a mutual pursuit of God's purpose for their lives.

Family Dynamics

Getting to know each other's families is an integral part of waiting on God's timing. Family dynamics can reveal a great deal about your partner's upbringing, values, and character. Observing how your partner interacts with their family members, and hearing stories about their background, can offer a deeper understanding of who they are beyond the courtship phase. This insight is invaluable as it helps to see the influences that have shaped your partner's personality and behavior. Family interactions can highlight important aspects such as respect, conflict resolution, and affection, which are critical to understanding your partner more comprehensively.

Additionally, spending time with your partner's family provides an opportunity to assess your own comfort level within their family environment. Since marriage involves merging families, feeling at ease with your partner's family is essential for a harmonious future. This experience allows you to see potential family dynamics and expectations that could impact your relationship. For example, understanding family traditions, communication styles, and expectations for holidays or gatherings can prepare you for future interactions and help you determine how well you fit into their family culture.

While family input shouldn't dictate your decision entirely, it serves as an important factor in discernment. Families often provide perspectives and insights that you might not see from within the relationship. Their observations can be invaluable in highlighting both strengths and potential challenges in your relationship. Listening to their feedback with an open heart can help you make a more informed decision about your future together. It's crucial to balance their input with your own experiences and feelings, ensuring that your final decision aligns with God's will and your personal convictions.

Engaging with each other's families also allows for deeper bonding and understanding between you and your partner. By witnessing how your partner treats and respects their family, you gain a clearer picture of their values and how they might approach your future family. Moreover, it provides a platform for discussing how you both envision blending your families and establishing your own family traditions. This process, when approached thoughtfully and prayerfully, can affirm your compatibility and readiness for a lifelong commitment, aligning your courtship with God's timing and purpose.

Patience Through Adversity

God's timing often involves presenting challenges and obstacles along the journey of courtship. These experiences are not meant to deter us but to refine our character, deepen our faith, and strengthen the relationship. They serve as tests of our commitment and resilience, revealing the true nature of our bond. James 1:2-4 reminds us, "My brethren, count it all joy when ye fall into divers temptations; Knowing this, that the trying of your faith worketh patience. But let patience have her perfect work, that ye may be perfect and entire, wanting nothing." These trials, though difficult, are instrumental in shaping a robust and enduring relationship that can withstand future challenges.

These trials teach us valuable lessons in patience, trust, and perseverance, which are crucial foundations for a successful marriage. When faced with obstacles, couples have the opportunity to rely on each other and on God's guidance, fostering a deeper sense of unity and dependence on divine wisdom. The process of overcoming these hurdles together strengthens their bond and builds a foundation of mutual respect and understanding. Romans 5:3-4 states, "And not only so, but we glory in tribulations also: knowing that tribulation worketh patience; And patience, experience; and experience, hope." This scriptural wisdom underscores how enduring trials can ultimately cultivate hope and resilience in a relationship.

Just as nature unfolds slowly and deliberately, God's timing unfolds in ways that are purposeful and meaningful. Rushing through courtship may lead to missed lessons and unpreparedness for the complexities of marriage. Embracing God's timing means accepting that each step of the journey has its purpose, whether it's to reveal a hidden character trait, teach a valuable lesson, or strengthen the couple's faith. Ecclesiastes 3:1 beautifully captures this truth: "To every thing there is a season, and a time to every purpose under the heaven." Recognizing the seasons in a relationship allows couples to grow through each phase with patience and grace.

Embracing patience allows couples to grow individually and together, preparing them for a lifetime commitment rooted in faith and mutual understanding. Through the trials and waiting periods, partners develop a deeper appreciation for each other's strengths and weaknesses, learning to support and uplift one another. This period of growth and refinement ensures that when the time for marriage comes, the relationship is built on a solid foundation of enduring love and unwavering faith. As Isaiah 40:31 assures us, "But they that wait upon the Lord shall renew their strength; they shall mount up with wings as eagles; they shall run, and not be weary; and they shall walk, and not faint." Waiting on God's timing empowers couples to enter marriage with renewed strength and confidence, ready to face life's challenges together.

Courting Timetable

While patience is virtuous, it's also important to maintain a reasonable timeframe for courtship. Typically, a courting period between six months to four years allows sufficient time to build a solid foundation of friendship, trust, and compatibility before marriage. This timeframe provides ample opportunity to navigate various aspects of the relationship, including compatibility in values, goals, and spiritual alignment. During this period, couples can learn to understand each other deeply and assess how well they complement each other's strengths and weaknesses, which is crucial for a successful marriage.

Striking a balance between patience and practicality ensures that couples honor God's timing while making informed decisions about their future together. A period of one to three years is often considered optimal for courtship, as it provides enough time to truly get to know each other without dragging the process unnecessarily. This balanced approach helps prevent potential frustrations or doubts that might arise from a prolonged period of uncertainty. It also ensures that both partners are genuinely committed to discerning God's will for their relationship, rather than merely prolonging the courtship out of indecision or fear of commitment.

It shouldn't take longer than four years to decide if you want to marry someone. If a couple has not reached a decision about marriage within this timeframe, it may indicate underlying issues or uncertainties that need to be addressed. While there are valid reasons for extended courtship, such as waiting for one partner to grow mentally and emotionally or to overcome specific challenges, it's essential to remain mindful of the relationship's overall direction and health. Continually evaluating the purpose and progress of the courtship helps ensure that both partners are moving forward with clear intentions and shared goals.

After four years, people's intentions and commitment levels may begin to be questioned. If, after such a lengthy period, there is still uncertainty about marriage, it might be a sign that the person is not the right fit. It's crucial to have open and honest conversations about the future and to seek God's guidance in these decisions. Prolonging the courtship without a clear purpose can lead to frustration and doubt. Therefore, being decisive and intentional within a reasonable timeframe helps build a relationship that is grounded in faith, mutual respect, and a shared vision for the future.

I have a relative who was in an on-and-off relationship for five years. His girlfriend wanted to marry him, but he was always uncertain. After three years, he finally proposed, only to call it off when he met another woman who piqued his interest even more. When that new relationship didn't work out, he returned to his former fiancée and decided to commit to her, reasoning that "at least she's not crazy." However, on a trip soon after, he met yet another woman who captivated him, leading him to break off his engagement a second time and get engaged to this new person. This cycle of indecision and shifting commitments highlighted his underlying doubts and the lack of a deep, enduring connection with his long-time girlfriend.

His hesitation to marry his ex-fiancée for five years stemmed from loving her but not feeling that powerful, in-love sensation that solidifies long-term commitment. Doubts and uncertainties can serve as important signals in a relationship, indicating underlying issues that might not be immediately apparent. Ignoring these doubts or trying to push through them can lead to prolonged emotional turmoil and repeated cycles of indecision. It's crucial to listen to these internal warnings, as they often reflect genuine concerns about compatibility and longterm happiness.

A life with someone is a long journey, and entering into marriage should be a decision made with confidence and clarity. When you have persistent doubts, they could signify deeper issues that need to be addressed before making such a significant commitment. Often, when you know, you know—especially for men. This certainty forms the foundation of a strong, enduring partnership. Ignoring doubts or settling out of convenience or fear of being alone can lead to future heartbreak and regret. It's better to be honest with oneself and one's partner, ensuring that the commitment to marriage is made with full assurance and mutual understanding.

Bonus Tip

In the dynamics of romantic relationships, a biblical perspective often emphasizes that the man should be the one to chase. This view is grounded in scripture, such as Proverbs 18:22, which states, "He who finds a wife finds what is good and receives favor from the Lord." This suggests that men are naturally inclined, by divine design, to pursue and initiate romantic connections. When a woman chases a man, even if he accepts her advances, it may be more out of convenience rather than genuine affection or desire, potentially leading to an imbalance in the relationship dynamics. By following this biblical principle, relationships can align more closely with God's intended order.

Women may sometimes feel a strong urge to chase after a man they truly like, but it's often advised to resist this impulse. If a man shares the same feelings, he will naturally take the initiative to pursue the woman. When a man is genuinely interested, he will go to great lengths to win her over, demonstrating his commitment and dedication. By allowing a man to be the pursuer, a woman can gauge his true level of interest and commitment. She can certainly drop subtle hints and show her interest, but ultimately, the man's pursuit is a key indicator of his genuine feelings.

While this approach may not apply universally and there are certainly exceptions, it is generally observed that relationships tend to be more balanced and fulfilling when the man takes on the role of the pursuer. If a man does not pursue, it might be an indication that the relationship is unlikely to thrive. Therefore, adhering to this traditional dynamic can often lead to stronger, more stable romantic connections. Nonetheless, it's important to recognize that each relationship is unique, and what works best can vary greatly depending on individual personalities and circumstances.

www.ingramcontent.com/pod-product-compliance
Lightning Source LLC
Chambersburg PA
CBHW071006120626
46546CB00003B/964